FROM RAGS TO RICHES

Children's Home
Boarding Schools
USMC Vietnam
Fire Department Captain
Sheriff's Deputy

WILBUR WHITE

authorHOUSE

AuthorHouse™
1663 Liberty Drive
Bloomington, IN 47403
www.authorhouse.com
Phone: 833-262-8899

Published by AuthorHouse   07/28/2022

ISBN: 978-1-6655-6674-2 (sc)
ISBN: 978-1-6655-6673-5 (hc)
ISBN: 978-1-6655-6672-8 (e)

Library of Congress Control Number: 2022913950

Contents

Acknowledgements

Thanks to my wife, Elsa Lee, for making this book possible through her encouragement, dedication and hard work. She kept me writing (all by hand) and made the story flow. She was the brains behind the whole thing; and without her, the story of my life would not have been told.

Thank you, Connie, my baby girl, for taking such interest in all we do, and to her husband Glenn for loving me in spite of all the harassment I give him. And thanks to our grand children, John Thomas and Jamie Lee, and her husband Derrick, and our great grandson, Austin Lee-Louis. You are terrific kids. You make our lives so rich and beautiful with your love.

Thanks to Adrienne and Megan our granddaughters by marriage, for bringing us much joy. And Thanks to Megan and Joe for bringing us so much sweetness we can hardly stand it through those beautiful twins, Molly and Marie.

I also thank my brothers and sisters and scores of friends who reminded me of events that helped me get the details straight. And special thanks to my sister Emma who shared sequential parts of our lives. She allowed me to use dates and events from her Memoires, "AS I WAS TOLD", which she had already written.

Also, thanks to our next-door neighbors, Bob and Francis Edwards, who heard some of these real-life escapades and kept hounding me to get this done.

Thanks to my wonderful, long time friend, Clara Craig, for editing this book and making me sound smart and intelligent. Clara is a perfectionist and she cringes when she reads books with mistakes. In some cases, I insisted on improper grammar when I thought it suited my narrative. Don't blame her for that.

Finally, the most important person in my life is my Lord and Savior, Jesus Christ. Without Him, as you will see in the book, this story would have a very different outcome. He is present in all we do, and that's why Lee and I have enjoyed a beautiful life together these past 57 years.

PART 1

Faith Children's Home

Birth Family
Children's Home
Early Schooling

1

They loved the new PJs

We always sang

6th grade
Southside Elem, Beattyville, Ky

2

The White family taken in ten months ago. Their mother passed away ~~████████████~~

BEAR TRACK BIBLE MISSION
Faith Childrens Home
REV. and MRS. JACK BROWN
Route 1
Beattyville, Kentucky

NO ADOPTIONS — — — — — — — NO SOLICITORS

A WORK OF FAITH

Henry   Preacher   Homer
              Bill

Bobby, Emma, Johnny, Wilbur, Edna, Joyce, Jr

Daddy's Funeral. Irvine. KY

I remember the day Jack Brown from the Faith Children's Home at Bear Track, Kentucky, came to Pryse, Kentucky, to get us at Grandma and Grandpa White's house. The hog lot was just below the house, and in the yard was a cherry tree that hung out over the pig pen. This is where I was found--up in that tree over the pig pen. If I had had a tail, I would have been a monkey because later my nickname was "Monkey Lee." (My middle name is Lee.)

Finally, after many promises of the good times I would have with other kids and the chance to ride a bike, they coaxed me out of the tree and into the pickup truck that was to transport five of us seven children to our new place to live. This was the best thing that ever happened to us though we did not know it at the time. My dad was a widower and a lover of alcohol. He worked long hours on the railroad and could not deal with seven children ages 16 months to 11 years.

I remember very little about my mother, Ella Dee McIntosh White. She was only 29 years old with seven children when she died of "consumption" (tuberculosis is what they call it now) on March 12, 1951. She was buried at the Pinnacle Cemetery at Old Landing in Lee County, Kentucky. All of us kids were taken for testing and were advised that we would take the recommended medications and were not to take the common tuberculosis test. All of us, as far as I know, had chest x-rays since the skin test came back with a "false positive." None of us got tuberculosis.

I vaguely remember knowing Mom being sick and seeing her lying in bed by the fireplace. She knew she was dying. She told Daddy to "keep the kids together." He did the best he could under the circumstances, but there was no way he could care for us all by himself.

Sister Emma said that Mom was always a very clean housekeeper. I don't remember that; but to this day, all of us kids try to keep a clean house. I guess we got it from Mom.

We never got to know our aunts, uncles, and cousins from our mother's side of the family until recent years.

Daddy came to see us from time to time at the Children's Home and even took us home to live with him in the summers and on holidays. One year later, he married a lady named Anna Horn. Annie, as we called her, was the best stepmom anyone could ever have. She tried to get us back from the Children's Home to raise us, but Daddy still drank a lot; and they would not let us go back. Anna White was the hardest working person I have ever known. She loved us like we were her own, and we loved her. I don't think Daddy could have married a woman who would have loved him more. She was also very jealous and with good reason because Dad sometimes had a tendency to stray like the time he brought home a black lady from the bar. Now Annie was skinny and about five feet tall, but that woman left faster than she came in. What was he thinking?

In the summer we stayed with Annie and Daddy on Liberty Road in Lexington where the school bus garage is located now. We lived in a little white house with asbestos siding. This was a farm that was owned by a Mr. Griggs. He had some hogs and a big barn where they hung several acres of tobacco each year. Annie did laundry for Mr. Griggs and spent a lot of time at the ironing board.

Sometimes we got to spend time with our older and younger brothers who did not go to the Home. They stayed with Daddy's parents, Miriam and Harrison White, in Irvine. Bobby, who was the eldest son, went to Dayton to live with our uncle when he was eleven. Junior, the baby, was raised by our grandparents. Bobby learned to drink also, so he and Daddy would get drunk together and often threatened to kill each other with a gun.

We have lived in Joyland Park subdivision in Lexington since 1971. When I was a child, Daddy took us to the amusement park called Joyland that was in this area. We loved eating the cotton candy and riding the rollercoaster "all made of wood!" On one occasion, Daddy got drunk and left Annie, Edna, Joyce, and me to walk home to Liberty Road about five miles away. We walked about a mile, and someone picked us up and took us home.

Annie's brother, Roy Horn, worked at Dixie Bell Dairy in downtown Lexington at Third and Limestone streets. When my brother Johnny got older, he worked there, also; and they brought us big metal jugs with push-down lids filled with buttermilk with yellow flakes in it. Yum-Yum! It was so good.

One Sunday afternoon we were all playing in the yard and decided to do some "high jumping." Daddy almost busted a gut laughing when Johnny was ready to jump and slipped on the grass instead and ended up on the ground with one leg over the pole and the other foot under the pole. Later that same day, Johnny and I were running around the house in opposite directions. As we came around the corner, our heads banged together and almost knocked both of us out. I got mad when Johnny blamed it on me! He said that I was running too close to the house! We all laughed when I said he was running the same distance from the house that I was. We still laugh about it today.

Daddy worked on farms and did construction jobs to support his drinking and gambling habits. In spite of this, Annie loved him and was very jealous.

Annie was the one who was responsible for paying for the house and taking care of the bills. Without Annie, Daddy would probably not have had anything in this world. She was a great cook and was very thrifty with everything. She canned all the produce she could grow or buy. We never lacked for food when we were there. She lived through--or I should say survived--the Great Depression of 1929. As a result, she saved every bread sack and every piece of tin foil she could find. When preparing her house for sale after her death, we found coffee cans stuffed with bread sacks and tin foil pieces.

Daddy died on May 29, 1999, at 82 years of age from lung cancer that had gone to his brain. My wife, Lee, and I, being Power of Attorney, had to clear up all the bills and property. At the time Kentucky was just changing the laws, and we had to comply. Up until this change, the spouse could keep a car, a home, and $2,000 cash. Little did we know how this would affect us, but we did survive. When Daddy got sick, the University of Kentucky Medical Center did a lot of testing and medical procedures, such as penetrating his back to draw fluid off his lungs. Every procedure was a huge cost. Insurance, of course, only paid a portion of it all.

Annie was in control of things even though I was Power of Attorney, and she insisted that I pay the bills from all his medical care as they came in. I tried to get her to wait to give the insurance time to negotiate first; but she said, "I saved my money to take care of Elree." Therefore, I wrote the checks. We never got any money back from the hospital or the insurance company, although there were some bills we would not have been required to pay.

At that time Daddy had about $200 in his bank account. He had retired a few years earlier as custodian at the North Ashland Avenue Baptist Church. He had worked there for many years. Daddy had conquered all his bad habits by then and had become a Christian, but he was still stubborn and very selfish.

All the time that Daddy worked for the church, Annie babysat; and they lived in the parsonage and nursery on Ashland Avenue in front of the church. Annie saved her money and bought a house on Richmond Avenue where they lived before moving down to Cramer Avenue where Daddy "Pappy" died.

Shortly after Daddy died, Annie started getting sick with stomach and lower abdomen problems. We hired my sister Edna to come and live with her for a while as a live-in caregiver; but as Annie got worse, we took her to the Irvine Nursing Home because she wanted to be near her brothers who lived in Irvine. We sold the house (according to the state requirements) and used the money to take care of her in the nursing home in Irvine. Her brother Roy came every day for several years and fed her lunch as long as he was physically able. After she went to the nursing home, Annie refused to sit up or to walk. She was bedfast the entire time. One day the nurse met me outside and said that Annie had quit eating and had told them she was dead. I walked into Annie's room and spoke to her, but she wouldn't respond. Finally, she told me that she was dead. She kept her eyes shut and her hands folded across her chest. She lived a few years after this incident. Both Daddy and Annie are buried in South Irvine, Kentucky.

All the time I was growing up I thought that I was born in Pryse, Kentucky. This is a small village just a little southeast of Irvine and Ravenna, Kentucky. But after talking with my sister and remembering some small things about my childhood, I think that was not so. I do not remember anything about Old Landing where Mom is buried, which is just outside Irvine; but we are pretty sure that is where I was born.

I do, however, remember the section houses at Pryse. Our house was just below the railroad tracks and very close to them. I could climb up on the porch and pee on the tracks. I remember I had a bed in the corner of the house. When my door was open and there was a fire in the Warm Morning stove, I could see the light from the fire flickering on the wall from the vents in the stove door. It is such a little thing but so relaxing and comforting.

There is one other thing I remember at this section house. My sister Edna, who is two years younger than I, and I were playing a game. She put her index finger on the edge of the porch, and I tried to hit it with my hammer, which was, actually, a heavy piece of steel that we used for a door stop. She did not move it fast enough, and I have always had a good aim. Her finger is still flat! In a round-about way, that came back to haunt me when I got the end of my finger cut off in shop class in high school! Edna has a flat index finger, and I have a slightly stubby index finger! Enough said about that!

We next moved to Irvine, Kentucky, at White Oak out on Winchester Road. We had to cross the creek with no bridge to get to our house up on the hill. We played on that hill and on the road leading down to the creek. The creek was not deep at this point, but sometimes it was rutted and impassible after a rain. I remember rolling up into a ball inside an old tire, someone gave it a push, and I rolled down the hill toward the creek.

There was also a lot of clay in the ground around there, and we made a slingshot with an old shoe tongue and some rubber from an old inner tube. Red rubber was the best. (I was told that is what David used to kill Goliath.) Then we rolled that clay into small balls about three-fourths inch diameter. We next put them on a flat pan and baked them in the oven to get hard. They worked well in the slingshot.

We moved back to Pryse from White Oak and lived in a white house on the left of the road, up a small incline. Grandma Miriam and Grandpa Harrison had already moved back to Pryse and lived in a house just below the road toward the railroad tracks, about a hundred yards from our house. Grandpa had a Model A Ford, but he could not drive it. He could not work the clutch and spark advance and gas to make them work together. Daddy had to drive it wherever they went.

I remember the ice truck coming around with ice for our icebox to preserve our food. That truck had a wooden bed with a heavy tarp on top so the ice would not melt. The ice man used an ice pick to break off the size you wanted. This was right after the war, and there was a shortage of metal. We collected any scrap metal we could find to make a few pennies to spend on a treat.

I remember Daddy going squirrel hunting, and squirrel made a great supper. Mom knew she was going to die and said if she died that night, she would be full because she had eaten a big supper. She had gotten sick after hanging clothes out on the line a few days before. According to Emma, my oldest sister, the last thing she said was, "Elree, keep the children together." I'm sure Daddy did the best he could.

When I decided to join the Marines in 1964, I needed a birth certificate which I had never had to have before because I was born at home with a midwife doing the honors. Daddy took me to Frankfort to get one made. Everyone had always called me "Wilbur," but Daddy said he had named me "Wilburn," with an "n," and that's what he called me till he died. When we got the birth certificate made, I spelled it "Wilbur," so now it is official.

Back to the Children's Home –

Daddy Brown was not perfect; I can tell you this from experience. They were building a concrete block building that was to become the living quarters for the boys and girls and was also going to be used for Sunday School and church. One day Daddy Brown let me play with the measuring tape. When I finished with it, someone else got it and broke it. I did not know this; but when Daddy Brown found it broken, it was only right that he thought I did it. No matter what I said, I could not convince him that I knew nothing about it. You can guess what happened, and it was hard to sit down for a while.

When we first arrived at the Children's Home to stay, I got into the car and locked all the doors. I don't remember how they bribed me to get out. Probably it was with food and riding bikes. Later in the day I cried and told my sister Emma ("Sissy"), "Let's go home before it gets dark." She said it broke her heart to tell me that this was our home now. She was only nine years old at the time.

The house we lived in was maybe 2,500 square feet with an upstairs and a basement where the laundry was done. Some of the boys lived down there as well. We had one old wringer washer, and all the clothes were hung outside to dry on the clothesline. Washing clothes was a continuous process. Gertie, Ruthie, Shirley, and all the older girls were always washing clothes. Imagine if you had to do laundry for thirty-six kids and about twelve or more were in cloth diapers. There were no disposable diapers at that time. When a baby made a mess, you scraped it out, rinsed the diaper, and put it in the large tub of bleach water to get ready for the next laundry day.

We made lye soap in a large iron kettle out in the yard. The hot liquid was then poured into a pan where it hardened. Then it was cut into chunks measuring about two by three inches. When the girls did the laundry, they scraped the soap into the washer. Sometimes a small piece of soap didn't dissolve in the water and ended up in a fold in some of our clothes. Several times at school I unfolded a place in my shirt and found a small piece of soap.

Many times, the boys' shirts and the girls' dresses were made from the feed sacks that the feed for our chickens and other animals came in. Skirts for the girls were often made from flour sacks. They were made with nice patterns for that purpose. Those sacks were sewn together with thread that you had to learn how to unravel without destroying the sack or material. You simply got hold of the two strings, one on each side, and pulled from both sides of the sack. It would unravel without tearing the sack.

We ate and cooked on the main floor of the house. The kitchen went almost all the way across the house. On the opposite side of the house were a couple of small rooms used for different things. There was a fireplace at the front of the house, and outside was a porch that went the length of the house with steps leading down to the play area. At the other end of the house was a small room at the end of the kitchen. Also, there was a stairwell going down to the basement, and in one corner of the house was a small bathroom.

One thing I distinctly remember is that under the kitchen cabinets was a large five-gallon can with "cracklings" in it. These were pork rinds that had been rendered by putting them in the oven and baking the grease out or by boiling them over the outside fire in a large black kettle. The grease that was rendered out was called "lard," and that is what we cooked with. No vegetable oil or specialized "canola" or "peanut" oils for us!

The upstairs had a dividing wall with the boys on one side and the girls on the other. We also had girls' and boys' toilets outside. The reason I tell you this is that there were thirty-six boys and girls living in this space.

Concerning these outhouses--they had to be moved from time to time for obvious reasons. We tried not to put things down there that didn't belong because of filling them up too soon. Well, one of the kids threw a can in one hole. Miss Anna Lee, who helped with the children at the Home, found it but could not find the guilty party. While questioning all of us boys, she asked Raleigh how big the can was. He showed her with his hands. He was caught! These were learning experiences. Either you did not do it, or at least you shouldn't give out information concerning the act.

When I was about seven years old, I was skinny and probably weighed 75 or 80 pounds. This made me a prime candidate for a problem that occurred in the girls' toilet. It seems that one of the older girls had false teeth; and somehow, they had fallen out of her mouth and landed about four feet down the hole. I was just tall enough that when they held me by my feet, I could reach those teeth in that stuff. I'm glad they had a good grip on me, or I would have had a crappy outlook on life!

Some of this next story is not true, but it's funny, nevertheless. At the last house we lived in we had a four-seater toilet. We never needed psychological therapy because we could communicate with each other while relieving ourselves. When they put a commode inside the house, we didn't know how to operate it. When we came in from the cornfield or working in the garden, we just put one foot in this thing and pushed a little handle down. It rinsed that foot and gave clean water for the other dirty foot. It had two lids on it, but we didn't know what they were for. We took them off, and Mama rolled biscuit and pie dough on the solid one. Then we framed Grandpa's picture in the one that had the hole. Everyone loved it. They said it looked just as natural as if he were sitting right there. We really did have a four-seater toilet.

The bathroom in the house was about eight-foot square and had a shower, a sink, and one commode. Now there was a lady who worked there to help take care of the kids. She cut our hair, gave us penicillin shots if we even looked sick, and did not spare the rod. Her name was Miss Anna Lee Mason from Tennessee.

When I first met Miss Anna Lee Mason, I had never had a shower in my life. We always used a No. 2 wash tub. When she and Mama Brown tried to put this little five-year-old boy in the shower, I thought they were trying to drown me. The fight was on. Later I learned that a shower was good for you, and we got a shower every Saturday night whether we needed it or not.

Another lady, Aunt Mable Trott, was our schoolteacher. She read us stories after our showers and always left us wanting more. We could not wait till next Saturday night to finish the story. She also cut our fingernails and toenails. I don't think any of these people were paid-- maybe just room and board--but oh what treasures in Heaven they have. There was also a man named Jim Pew who helped on the farm. Yes, we had many acres and raised a large garden. We had a horse or two, cows for milk, hogs, and chickens. We raised the best tomatoes in the world! What made them taste so good was when we knocked a corner off a livestock salt block and rubbed it on the tomatoes and ate them out in the field. I think the cow saliva made them even better!

Now one day Daddy Brown and Jim Pew were about seven feet down in a well digging it out so we could catch the water from the roof for our household needs. Jimmy Sipple and I were standing on the edge looking down, and I got off balance and started flailing my arms. Before I fell, I grabbed hold of Jimmy and took him in with me, right on top of those guys' heads. Thank goodness no one was hurt.

Jim Pew was a good old man and was a big help around the Home- -in the garden, working the farm, or wherever he was needed. He was always there. He did have a problem that I remember well. He passed gas a lot. He told my brother Johnny that he hoped he didn't do that when he grew up. Now the one thing that all of us remember is that every morning Jim Pew prayed so loud that we could hear his voice ring out all over those hills. Mr. Pew was happy, but he had very few assets in this old world. He lived in a room that was made for him in an old log barn. I will see him in Heaven.

When I was about seven years old, I had a small wart in the corner of my mouth. Mr. Ed Phillips, who lived near the Home at the end of the driveway, told me to find an old bone, rub it on that spot, turn around, throw the bone over the hill, and forget about it. Well, a few days later when I found a bone near the driveway, I remembered what he had told me. I rubbed it on the wart, turned around, threw that thing over my shoulder down the hill, and forgot about it. In about two weeks that wart was gone! We don't know where Mr. Ed got his medical training, but maybe he could give some doctors some useful insights today. Just saying.

One time I had a swing in the driveway of the barn. As I was swinging, a calf with little horns ran in under me and stopped after I had just gone forward! You can imagine what happened next. What could I do? Nothing. I still have the scar on my backside to prove it!

We learned how to live, work, and play. We all had jobs and responsibilities. One of my jobs when I was about eight years old was to cut kindling for the stove. I still have a scar on my left index finger to remind me of that.

At nine years old I was sent to the woods by myself with a double-bladed ax and a file to cut locust posts for fences. I don't remember getting hurt while doing that; I just learned by doing.

I was just a little skinny guy who could climb a tree and swing from the limbs like a monkey. I was always jumping to or hanging from tree branches, or standing on my head, even on a fence post at the corner of the fence in the school yard. In 1951 baseball shoes had metal spikes. I found a pair that was probably too big for my feet, but I got them on. I could run halfway up a tree with those things and grab a limb and swing or climb. This is very evident in our home videos that we watch now where I am swinging upside down by my knees from a limb or a swing like Forrest Gump. He must have learned that from me.

Oh, how I loved the meringue they put on the top of our pies. One time at the barn I got some eggs, a bowl, and a corn cob for a whip and tried to make my own meringue. I forgot that I needed sugar and heat to get that good delicious brown look. It did not work out very well.

I don't know why, but I loved canned dog food; and I often stole it out of the storage room and ate it. I did that several times until I started chasing cars and howling at the moon! Ha! Ha! I really did eat that dog food, but I don't know where we would have gotten canned dog food since it would be more expensive than dry food.

I was always hungry, and I used to sneak out of bed at night and go to the kitchen to find something to eat. This was just the child in me, because the Browns and God always fed us well. We had everything we needed. Daddy and Mama Brown were the most dedicated, hardworking, and loving people on God's green earth. Sometimes the Game Warden would stop by the house and bring us a "road-kill" deer. I guarantee it did not go to waste around that place.

Now, we were not picky about what we ate. If they set it in front of us, we ate it. There were no warnings on food packages. I don't think that cholesterol had been invented yet, because if we had had any we would have fried it and eaten it. And we didn't know what "wind chill factor" was either. We knew when we were hot or cold. But now, if they say it is a little cool and you step outside, you can freeze to death if the wind is blowing a little! They say the wind chill only affects living things like humans and animals, so I guess we just get smarter all the time.

I made a bow and arrow one time out of a limb from the big willow tree just below the house. It was so powerful that Miss Anna Lee would not let me bring it past the barn because it was too dangerous to have around other people.

I smoked rabbit tobacco made from a weed that grew out in the field. We used a brown paper sack to roll these. We also tried to smoke grapevines, but they burned our tongues. If we had other kinds of drugs, I'm sure we would have tried them, too. Daddy Brown purchased a gas tank to hold gas for our farm equipment; and I found that if I sucked on the hose, it made a rattle or buzz noise. It also made me dizzy and was exciting to do because it made me get high. This only happened for about a month; then I didn't do it any longer. I guess when we are young, we have to experiment.

Miss Anna Lee was a disciplinarian and loved to keep us in line. She used a belt or switch, but that was not what hurt so bad. It was her fingernails that dug into my underarm that really hurt. We went around in circles as she whipped me with a switch that someone else had gotten for her because the one she sent me after was not big enough or stout enough. I wasn't stupid. When I was about eight years old, I was smart about some things, like fetching my own switch, as I just explained. So, one time I brought her back a handful of rocks and asked her if she could just "stone me" instead. It didn't work either.

Finally, I did get her sympathy when I got stung by a bunch of yellow jackets after some of the boys convinced me to take a hoe and spread a brush pile so they could burn it. Being the obedient kid I was, I never saw any harm in it. Just as I hit that pile of brush, those yellow jackets swarmed all over me. I threw that hoe down and started running as the bees were stinging me all over my body. I could not get close to those boys because they knew they would get stung. You couldn't have caught them on a motorcycle. I got a lot of care and sympathy from Miss Anna Lee for a few days as I lay out on the porch swelled up so much that I was barely recognizable. I'm certainly glad my three angels were there and that I was not allergic to all those stings.

Now at one point when we were about nine years old, Donald Johnson and I swept and dust mopped the second floor of the block building that we had built. We did this once a week on Saturday. In fact, on Saturdays, Miss Anna Lee would assign Donald and me several jobs to do. Most of the time I completed most of my jobs, but Donald would get involved with other things and not do his. I got punished for not doing his work, but I was not even aware what his assignments were. This did not matter to Miss Anna Lee. She whipped me as we went around and around with me yelling, "No more, no more." She asked me why I did not do the work, and I would say, "I forgot." Then she said, "I don't want to ever hear you say that you forgot." Therefore, the next time I said, "I didn't remember." She still spanked me!

Anna Lee Mason purchased a house a couple hundred yards down the road from the main house. Tubby, Donald, and I lived with her for a while before I started going to boarding schools. Tubby slept downstairs, and Donald and I slept in the attic on each side of the big double doors that led out onto the roof. On Saturday night we watched *Gunsmoke* and *Bonanza*. Then we said our prayers and went up the pull-down stairs to the attic. I always said the same prayer, and I think it did work. My prayer was, "Dear Jesus, help Miss Anna Lee, Mama, Daddy, and Aunt Mable. Thank you for our food. Amen." I don't remember what Donald said, but it was basically the same. One night he got mixed up and said something wrong. He stopped and then started again with "I mean" and continued his prayer. I laughed out loud, and that night my bottom was a little warm when I went to bed.

Miss Anna Lee loved her animals. She had a pig named Penny, some geese, chickens, and turkeys. Down on one side of the pig lot was a sycamore tree that had a low limb. Penny, the pig, knew about the low limb; and when I rode her around the lot, or at least halfway around, she always ran under that same sycamore tree and dragged me off on the low limb. Miss Anna Lee's old gander used to hiss and try to bite me. One day I hit him with a board and knocked him unconscious. I thought I had killed him, and I was in trouble for sure, but he came to. What a relief!

I used to carry a five-gallon bucket of slop from the main house to Anna Lee's house to slop the hogs. I was good at swinging the bucket around me as I walked, and it helped pull me along.

After the chores were done, we caught the bus to school at Yellow Rock, which was a one-room school on top of a hill. (Recently we revisited the area, and there is no sign of the school building nor the line-houses at the bottom of the hill.) Part of my second grade was at this school; then I went to Beattyville Elementary. My next school was Heidelberg Elementary School where I stayed until I switched to Southside Elementary in sixth grade.

I failed the second grade at Beattyville, but I'm sure that stealing the teacher's apple from the coat room had nothing to do with my failing that year. I was hungry; I was always hungry.

There was a boy in my class who was in love with the same girl as I, and we fought over her. Carol was her name, and she was beautiful. As a matter of fact, the school got us some boxing gloves and put us in a ring up on stage for an assembly program one morning and let us go at it. I think I whipped him because I knocked him out of the ring. Actually, I probably pushed him out. Then again, he probably thinks he won. Who knows? We really were friends, but we just happened to love the same girl. This is the same guy, Jimmy Sipple, that I pulled into the well with me. Now you know why I did it.

(NOTE – It has been many years since these school days, and I may be confused on some dates and there are no school records to confirm or deny as the old house burned many years ago.}

I had several experiences at Heidelberg. One day the school bus threw a rod coming down the hill at Heidelberg, and a piece of the rod came through the hood of the bus. Fortunately, no one was hurt.

The Heidelberg school had wooden floors, and the janitor cleaned the floors with used sawdust mixed with oil. Do you remember the smell when we returned to school in the fall after the wood plank floors had been oiled? I do. Talk about a fire hazard!

We used to play marbles for keeps if we didn't get caught. There was a bank about twelve feet tall beside our outside toilet. One day I got into a fight with one of the boys while standing at the edge of this bank. I'm glad we didn't fall off it. Anyhow, he tore all the buttons off my feed-sack shirt. I knew that when I got home, I would be in big trouble. I looked at him in disbelief; and as I stood there crying, I reached and grabbed his shirt and ripped off all his buttons. The principal was Haggar Holland.

One day some of my friends got into trouble, and Mr. Holland led them up the school steps to his office for some discipline. Our lunchroom was in a building not connected to the school, and I was standing by the corner. I hollered, "Hey, Haggar Holland, leave them boys alone." I had a hard time sitting down for a day or two. I never spoke to Principal Holland like that again. See, I was learning all the time.

My sixth grade started at Southside Elementary where I had a great teacher, Mrs. Maxie Roland. She cared about her students and tried to teach me the best she could. I also had a male teacher there, but the only thing I remember about him is that he taught us how to waltz. He was probably the music teacher. What I enjoyed most about school was going outside and dusting the erasers.

Anyway, back to the Children's Home. With thirty-six kids in one house and four staff, we were tight.

Christmas only came once a year, but oh what a wonderful time we had! Well, most of the time; except the time I caught Santa's beard in my new flying saucer!

There was a business in downtown Lexington called Taylor Tire. I think all the employees and owners attended the same church because they came to the Children's Home with large boxes containing many presents. This was good new stuff like we had never seen before. They always brought Santa with them. We had toys, wrappings, and boys and girls all over the floor. Then it snowed, and we all pulled our "High-Flyer" sleds--or ones we made for the occasion--and went to the fields to slide down the hills. We built snowmen and forts which we hid behind and threw snowballs at the girls as they came out the back door of the house.

Those people at Taylor Tire were the most wonderful and loving individuals God put on this earth. I am sure they never knew the joy they brought to this Eastern Kentucky family at Bear Track, Kentucky, eight miles from Beattyville. As a matter of fact, in 1968 when I was discharged from the USMC, my wife, Lee, and I made Lexington our home. One day I stopped at Taylor Tire and shared this story with the folks. I thanked them for the joy they brought to Faith Children's Home in the 1950s.

All of the staff members at the Youth Haven Bible Camp where we went every summer were so very entertaining for us kids. The women told stories and did skits while we were eating. I remember one story that Aunt Martha related about being on a train and a man robbed it. He told all the passengers to put their money, rings, and all their jewelry into the bag he was holding. Aunt Martha said, "Aunt Gladys, too?" The robber said, "You heard me, you heard me." Then he said he was going to go around and kiss all the ladies. Aunt Martha said, "Aunt Gladys, too?" Then Aunt Gladys said, "You heard him, you heard him!" We always laughed and laughed. It is a wonder we didn't get choked from laughing so hard since this was always while we were eating.

The camp was such a good place for young people to get trained. In the lunchroom we used large metal trays with compartments and silverware which had to be cleaned. It was our responsibility to clean them after every meal. There were large tubs of hot water outside with soap and a little mop to wash with. Then we moved down the line to the rinse tub.

At the camp we also got to use the band saws even at a young age. But, of course, there was always supervision. We also were allowed to use rubber molds and plaster of Paris to make our art masterpieces before we painted them.

We had Bible study, games, competitions, and worship time together. What a wonderful childhood I had because of the Children's Home and the Bible Camp that was on top of the hill next to our Home. Daddy Brown gave them the first five acres to start the camp. This camp is still doing great today with William Owens as director. We visit as often as we can and drive through the camp. I was speaker one night around their campfire, and several kids were saved. What an experience for me.

Pinecrest Youth Camp was another camp that we attended, and it was a couple of miles from the Home. Pinecrest was surrounded by very dangerous cliffs. Though we played games like "Capture the Flag" in the dark. (I'll introduce you to my protecting angels later), I can think of no one who was hurt due to these dangerous features of the land.

I did get hurt one time running in the dark when I ran into a concrete birdbath and loosened my front teeth. I was knocked unconscious. I was about ten years old at the time; and when I awakened, there was a beautiful girl bending over me looking in my face. That's when I knew I had lived a Christian life because I thought I had died and gone to Heaven. The girl was the daughter of Mr. Sperrow who owned the camp, and her name was Connie. She was about sixteen years old. Oh, and by the way, Lee let me name our daughter Connie because she looked like an angel, also.

I remember Daddy Brown taking trips to South Carolina to fill the back of the station wagon with peaches. He always took a couple of us boys with him to help pick them. We always put a wet blanket over the peaches filling the back of the station wagon so the fuzz from the peaches did not make us itch. Of course, he never had to pay for the peaches because he knew how to talk. Let me explain: One day close to Beattyville on Highway 52, a newly assigned state trooper stopped him for having no taillights. Not only did he not get a ticket, but the next day he was drinking coffee with the trooper and his wife at their house.

Daddy Brown did have some weaknesses when we were on these trips on the back roads, which were the only roads there were back then. When he saw the lights on at a ball field, he could not pass it up. So, there we would stop until the game was over. It never mattered who was playing. Fun for all!

When we arrived home with the peaches, the girls sat out in the driveway between the buildings and prepared them for canning. We had peach preserves all winter! Oh, how I'd love to have a jar of them now. I can still taste them. (Just let me insert this here: I was explaining this to my granddaughter, Jamie, and she wanted me to experience this again. So, she went home and made some. She gave me the first jar, and they are delicious! Thanks, Babe. You are a keeper.)

We farmed the land and raised vegetables. We had chickens and cattle and hogs. When we killed the animals, Mama Brown and the girls prepared the meat. We then took the meat to the Food Locker in Irvine which was designed to keep people's food in storage until it was needed. I'm pretty sure some of that "road-kill" deer was in there, too.

We had a black and white dog named Tip. I don't know what kind of dog he was, but someone told us that he was the kind that was used to pull sleds in Alaska. Well, one day I was sitting in the back seat of the car petting him. When I stopped, he bit me on the hand, so I jumped out of the car. The bite was not that bad, but I never did know why he bit me. However, he and I never had any problems before or after that incident. He was a good dog. Maybe he just had a headache.

Another time we had a dog named Rover. He was a collie and loved us kids, and we loved him. One day he went missing, and we had no idea where he was. The next day he returned with lots of energy and a good attitude. A few days later he left again, but he returned with a note pinned to his collar from a lady down the road. It said that Rover spent the night at their house and seemed to be okay even though he slept a lot. Mama Brown put a note on his collar that said we have thirty-six boys and girls in our house, and Rover probably just needed the rest.

We made go-carts out of a board, axles, and wheels; but there was no motor. One of our biggest problems was finding a large bolt and nut to attach in a way that we could steer the thing down the gravel road without running into the ditch. In my case, the ditch was not the problem; it was the fender of a '47 Ford that must have a dent in it from my head to this day. Talk about hardheaded; I've been that way since childhood.

We kids had great imaginations for creating toys. We didn't have a lot of things to play with like kids have today; no "fit-bits," individual wristwatches, or video games. We stomped empty tin cans, and the ends of the cans would fold up around our shoes. We used these for traction to climb the many banks and hills around the farm. We often took cardboard boxes and cut holes for windows and acted like we were driving a vehicle. It was so much fun, and we made noises like automobiles with our mouths. We were very creative back in the 1950s. Oh, for those simple days again. I am now 77 years old. Before very long, I might be making those noises again as my grandkids and great grandkids giggle and say, "Bless his heart!"

I started driving farm equipment and steering trucks while sitting on Daddy Brown's lap when I was about six years old. I drove the tractors before I had enough weight to push the clutch in, so to change gears I had to stand up and pull up on the steering wheel to push in the clutch.

Daddy Brown could do everything. He could overhaul a truck engine or replace transmissions in dump trucks. Often, I had to hold the transmissions in place while he bolted them in from underneath. I sat in the cab of the truck holding the transmission up by the gear shift. Daddy Brown always called me "Will." He said, "Where there's a 'Will,' there's a way." If I wasn't at the worksite, he would tell one of the boys to "go get Will."

We had four or five single-axle dump trucks, and each held about eight tons of rock. He paid employees about $8 a day to drive them. We hauled rock out of a rock quarry called Yellow Rock. The road coming out of Yellow Rock was a steep hill that dropped off drastically from the side of the road. The loaded truck coming out normally took the inside lane away from the drop off. One day one of our trucks reared up coming up the hill. It was a trick getting it back on four wheels, or should I say six wheels! Daddy Brown was driving the truck. Bobby Ray was riding in the truck with him and said, "I want down from here!" Better him than me; I only heard them tell the story many times.

Those trucks were kept busy for months hauling rock to Buckhorn Dam near Booneville, Kentucky. Daddy Brown and I would have some good conversations while I was riding shotgun with him.

We had a one-ton flatbed truck that we used in construction. This truck was a standard shift. One day we were in Beattyville on a street that had a pretty good incline. The parking lot was very steep and had about six inches of gravel on it. The truck was headed up hill. I was about thirteen years old, and Daddy Brown told me to get in the cab and pull the truck up. If you have ever tried to take off in loose, deep gravel on an incline, you know you are going to spin. I tried to ease out on the clutch to prevent this from happening. Twice I tried to coordinate the gas and clutch, but each time the motor died. I got frustrated and gave it a lot of gas, and the truck just sat there throwing gravel. Daddy Brown thought I was out of control; and when I put the clutch in, Daddy Brown was standing on the running board. Then he let me go ahead and get the truck out of that situation. It was like Lee's dad teaching her to drive. She ran the car into a disk-harrow that was parked in the field next to the driveway. He got out of the car and said, "You got it in here, you get it out." Then he went into the house. She figured it out, and he never mentioned the incident again.

Later, Daddy Brown built a blacktop plant close to the house; and we did driveways and parking lots in Irvine, Beattyville, and places in between.

We also farmed the land and raised corn and hay in places like Heidelberg and Millers Creek. At the end of the workday, we were very dirty. As we headed home from the fields, we stopped at the creek and took a dip with a bar of soap that Daddy always kept with him. The creek ran through a place called Sandfield. The highway crossed the creek at the bottom of the hill about one and a half miles from the Home. After our "bath" in the creek, we gathered horseweeds to take home to the hogs.

When I was six years old, I could not swim. The oldest boy in the home took me out on an inner tube in about seven feet of water and pushed me off. At that time, I didn't have an ounce of fat on me. I could walk across the bottom of a pool without floating. So, when he pushed me off the tube, I went straight to the bottom and was down there for some time. I'm not sure how long exactly. I remember crawling around on the bottom and could hear the water running over the rocks that were under the bridge. Now here is where God stepped in because I tried to open my mouth to breathe but could not open my mouth. I did not know what was going on above me, but Daddy

Brown was a very good swimmer. He dived in after me but had to go back up for air when he could not find me. He jumped in again to find me but was unsuccessful. However, this time I grabbed his foot--or at least God directed my hand to his foot--and he pulled me out as I was choking and spitting. I don't ever remember thanking Daddy Brown for saving me that day, but there are a lot of things I did not thank him for. "Thank you, Daddy and Mama Brown. The population of Heaven will be greater, because of your sacrifice, for so many families in Eastern Kentucky." I learned that I had three angels protecting me and their names were Surely (Shirley), Goodness, and Mercy . . . and they shall follow me all the days of my life...

I remember that Miss Anna Lee was one of the "smoke watchers" in the fire tower at the camp. I do not know how many years she took her shift, nor how long she stayed up there each shift. The tower was 95 feet tall, and one day I slid down the corner of that thing from top to bottom and had to sit on a chair for three hours. That was torture for me. I still have difficulty sitting still that long.

When I was about eight, I got an old guitar from somewhere and sat and plucked on it and tried to sing. Mr. Smallwood, a man from Sandfield, worked in the fire tower also. Well, he played guitar quite well and taught me to play the chords of G, C, and D. Those are the basic chords that I still play today. I would go up to an old empty chicken house on the hill above the main house to practice, and the chickens didn't seem to mind one bit. My fingers are short and do not have the dexterity as some do, but I still like to play rhythm guitar.

Our Children's Home began to grow. The older boys and girls moved to a house around the road about a quarter mile away, and the younger boys and girls stayed at the old place. I think I was the oldest boy left in the old house. This is where Miss Anna Lee ruled the roost, although her house was halfway between those two houses.

It is appropriate to stop here and move ahead about forty years. Miss Anna Lee Mason became a city police officer in Beattyville, Kentucky. She had powers of arrest, and, unlike Barney Fife (although about his size), she carried a fully loaded revolver. She absolutely knew how to use it. She wielded that revolver as handily as she did the belt! One day she shot a copperhead snake that was on Mama Brown's dresser!

The boy at the Home who was the oldest and meanest did not get along with Daddy Brown nor any of the other children. He is the one who almost drowned me. One time my brother Johnny knocked him out with a rubber boot. When I was about ten years old, this bully put me in a car and hooked a chain to a dump truck and dragged me in that car as I steered for about five miles. I was scared to death trying to drive that car with all the dust from the gravel road swirling around me. About this same time, he had a 22-caliber rifle. While shooting around my feet, he made me carry a 100-pound sack of feed about fifty yards from the house to the barn. I only weighed about 95 pounds. When I got to the barn, I threw that sack down and climbed to the top of the barn. He started shooting around me, and Bobby Johnson started throwing rocks at him. Then he started shooting at the boards of the barn that I was hiding behind. These boards were wide with wide cracks. If I had only had a rock!

Later, this boy was thrown out of the Navy; but we never learned why. I heard that in later years he straightened up and gave his life to the Lord. I certainly hope he did because he is my foster brother. His siblings were some of the best people you could ever meet. I respected Cecil, his brother, for he was very generous and kind. His sister Helen was killed in a motorcycle accident in Cincinnati, Ohio, in the 60s. His sister Ellen moved to California. However, the last we heard she had moved down south.

One day when I was about eleven, Mama Brown saw me driving the tractor on the highway from Beattyville. That's when I learned that husbands and wives don't always see eye to eye. But Daddy Brown never stopped letting us learn to do things even though they were sometimes risky. Once he accidentally laid his hand on a running chainsaw. He cut off the ends of his fingers and really messed up his fingernails. We learned by doing things, and usually no one got hurt badly. However, one time my brother Johnny fell off the tractor fender, and the sled they were pulling ran over his face. He sports a broken nose to this day!

We had lots of chickens, and we sold eggs in the area. Therefore, we had to have several chicken houses. When I was maybe twelve years old, we built a chicken house on the hill above the house. I cut the notch out of the rafter with a hatchet, so it could sit on the top plate of the wall.

At 77 years of age, I can still show you the scar on my left wrist where the hatchet ricocheted and made a slit about one and a half inches long and hit a nerve. Today when I press that area it gets numb.

We had some close calls, but I know the Lord was watching over us. That is what Mama Brown prayed every day. When we were building the two-story chicken house below the road, I was on top of the slightly sloping roof. As I walked across the rafters that I thought were nailed down, I discovered that the last one at the end of the building was not nailed down. When I bent over, I put my hand and weight on the loose rafter. It flipped right off the side of the building, and I flipped off right along with it for about thirteen feet. I landed on my feet beside a big stump, and the 2 x 6 board was bouncing all around my head. As a matter of fact, 13.5 feet is the height I was able to pole vault later at Annville Institute. I guess this incident was my training for pole vaulting.

We got to do a lot of target practice at those chicken houses—the target being rats. This was a lot of fun, and we learned to shoot well. This skill was nice to have when we needed to kill the chickens for the freezer. We used our 22-caliber rifles and killed probably twenty chickens at a time. I also learned that when you're chopping chickens' heads off, you need to use a straight-blade hatchet because a curved blade will probably not cut the heads off all the way, because you only get one hit. This was no fun!!

Mama Brown hated all guns with a passion! At one point, she got so fed up that she threw all the guns she could find down the well. Later, Daddy Brown was able to get them out. That is another example of husbands and wives not always seeing eye to eye.

We had lots of good times with our brothers and sisters. One day some of the boys were sawing logs to split for firewood. We poured some gasoline on a log and set it on fire. Then I ran in the house and told Ruth Brown that the guys sawed so fast that the log caught on fire. The look on her face when she saw it was worth it all. She was always the most gullible person I ever knew; you could make her believe anything. She later became a missionary and a schoolteacher. She was a wonderful person.

We were always learning new things like greasing the wheel barrel wheels or packing the wheel bearings for the dump trucks. This took practice. It required placing a big gob of grease in the palm of your hand and pressing the bearing into it until it was full. Oh, and we used the old bearings as taws when we played marbles. That sucker would hit those marbles, knock them out of the ring, and just sit there and spin. Then, you could keep shooting and clear the ring. Sometimes that taw would break the glass marbles. We played for keeps until we got caught.

At the Home we had lots of work going on constantly with lots of vehicle traffic. As a result, a lot of nails and sharp objects got lost on the ground. Daddy Brown had a standing order that for every nail we found, he would give us a penny. I don't ever remember receiving one cent though I found plenty of nails.

Daddy Brown was a man's man. He was about 6'3" and played baseball for the Beattyville baseball team. He was very competitive and encouraged us to be also. He was the same preacher who would not let us say things like darn, gee, golly, or anything off color. When he told Jimmy Johnson to move a chicken feed sack, Jimmy said that it had chicken shit on it. Without skipping a beat, Daddy Brown said, "Wipe it off." And he did, with a surprised look on his face, and kept on working.

This is the same man who punished us all. We had a large warehouse where we kept all types of tools to keep our equipment operating. One day Daddy Brown was trying to find a certain tool. After searching for some time, he could not find it. He assumed one of us eight boys present at the time had lost it so he lined us all up, took off his belt, and whipped each of us. About a half hour later, he found the tool right where he had put it. Then he called all of us boys back together, took his belt off, lined us up again, and said we all got one lick! I was the oldest boy there at the time, and I laid it on him. Don't you just hate people like that? That's why we had respect and love for him.

As you can imagine, we generated a lot of trash (including cans) at the Home. There was a large wooden box where we put the trash before we hauled it away. It was called the "can box." To dispose of this trash, we loaded it up and hauled it down the road to a pull off. We backed up to this pull off where there was a steep drop off. One of my biggest fears as a child was thinking we would drop over this cliff and die. I always tried to get out of the truck before it was backed up.

There were steep cliffs all around the property. We had some dogs that fell off a cliff, but only one child ever did. One day Ellen Hoskins fell off one of these cliffs onto the paved road below. She wasn't seriously injured. Thank God. Mama Brown told Lee and me that she prayed every day and said, "God, they're not mine today; they're yours, so watch over them for me."

When we were building the block building where a lot of us children moved to, there were large pieces of sheet metal for the duct work. Clifford Terry and I used some leftover pieces of the sheet metal and built a crude looking rectangle boat to use on the pond. We made paddles and became sailors until it started to sink. This boat only sat about four inches out of the water so you could not move around a lot. What made it even worse, it started to leak where we bent the metal in the corners. We mixed up some clay mud and stopped those holes up. It worked for a while. Fortunately, the pond wasn't that deep; and I had learned to swim by that time.

One time John Brown and I were experimenting and built a 22-caliber zip gun. We used a couple of small pipes with the bigger one surrounding the smaller one which was just big enough to hold a 22 bullet. This served as the barrel. The outside barrel had a little hole in it where we hooked a spring that we stretched back and attached to an Allen wrench. We had filed the end of the Allen wrench to form a little notch that served as a firing pin. This would strike the rim of the bullet causing it to fire. The Allen wrench worked well with this spring on it because it helped us to shoot straight. When we pulled back on the spring and put it in a bind, we could aim the gun better. Then all we had to do was push up on the Allen wrench to unbind it and let it slide forward striking the bullet. This worked very well except for one thing that had not entered the minds of these two 8-year-old boys. We set an empty Clorox bottle about four feet in front of us. We crouched on our knees, and John was behind me with only his right eye and right ear sticking out from behind my head. I triggered the zip gun and hit the bottle. Glass went everywhere, but it never touched me. However, a small sliver of glass struck John in his exposed ear; and I thought he was going to bleed to death! I don't know what happened to that gun, but we never shot it again. If Mama Brown found it, I am pretty sure it is still in the well!

Another true story is that John Brown and I used to watch a television show on our black and white set the size of a small icebox. *Sea Hunt* was a real adventure story with lots of emergency situations. The actor was Lloyd Bridges who played Mike Nelson on the show. The scene that stood out in our heads was him standing on the beach with all his scuba diving gear on including his flippers. To get the total adrenalin rush, John and I filled two 5-gallon buckets with water to see who could hold his head under the water the longest. I'm not sure who won, but we certainly had a good time. It was probably good for us. When I recently spoke with John about it, he said I always cheated! I can't imagine I would do such a thing. Shame on you, John, for accusing your brother. Actually, one time I did come up to take a breath and went back in, so it looked like I was still under when he came up gasping for air! You caught me that time, John. You scoundrel, you!

Mama and Daddy Brown's friends from California came for a visit. We automatically thought they knew everyone in California; or, at the least, they would know Mike Nelson. Well, they did not know Mike Nelson. John and I had a little conference and asked them about Lloyd Bridges. They said, yes, they did know him. So, we wrote a letter to Lloyd Bridges for these guests to carry back to California. It wasn't very long until John and I got a letter from Lloyd Bridges with a signed picture of him on the beach in his scuba gear. I can't tell you how exciting it was for two youngsters to receive a letter from Lloyd Bridges, aka Mike Nelson. We do not know what happened to the picture. Life just happens.

When I was around eleven years old, a newborn calf got tangled in the barbed wire fence and cut its stomach open. Its intestines were hanging out. I thought I could save it by sewing it up, so I got a needle and thread and went to work. It was cold that night, and I made a bed for the calf close to the furnace to keep it warm. I prayed it would live. At the time, my bed was in the basement not far from the furnace room. I heard the calf making noises all night. The next morning when I checked on it, I found it dead. I was so sad, but these are the kinds of experiences you have on a farm.

We try our best to keep in touch with all the siblings from the Children's Home. Lee and I send out letters to all whose addresses we have, and we meet for lunch each year at Blue Licks State Park or Natural Bridge State Park here in Kentucky on the Saturday following Labor Day.

There are many other tales to tell, but time and space are limited.

PART 2

Boarding Schools

Magoffin Institute
Riverside Christian School
Annville Institute

BEATTYVILLE ELEMENTARY SCHOOL

1961

Wilbur White

I was sitting here crying with salt and pepper in my eyes.

MAGOFFIN INSTITUTE THIS IS WHERE SATCHMO PULLED THE GUN ON ME AND MADE ME PRAY. IT WORKED.

15 yr old

17 YRS OLD

1964

Lincoln Hall,
Annville Institute

33

A s the children got older, Mama and Daddy Brown sent some of us to boarding schools. My brother Johnny went to Oak Dale near Jackson, Kentucky. My sister Emma "Sissy" went to Oneida in Clay County. Edna and Joyce went to Annville Institute in Jackson County. When I was thirteen years old in 1958, I was sent to Magoffin Institute in Breathitt County. This school was nine miles in either direction from a paved road. I don't know how much the Browns had to pay for us to live on those campuses, but I'm sure with Daddy Brown's ability to bargain it wasn't much. We also worked at the schools to help pay some of the cost.

At Magoffin Institute, I worked on the farm most of the time with two mules named Mert and Kate. The farm manager was Hardin Mullins. He taught me how to harness the mules and work them because the other kids did not want to do it. I enjoyed it because it was a challenge for me. I could drive that wagon through a gate with only a two- or three-inch clearance on each side. When we were in the field picking corn, the mules were an advantage over the tractor. When I needed the wagon to move up so I could throw the picked corn in the wagon, all I had to do was say "get up" or "whoa."

I also hauled the manure from the barn to the fields and garden. One day as I was spreading manure on the garden, I tried to throw a big pitchfork full off the side of the wagon. But the manure stuck to the pitchfork and jerked me off the wagon. I landed butt down right on top of a big cow pile.

I not only worked on the farm; I usually shoveled, by myself, eight tons of stoker coal from a truck into the bin for the furnace.

I learned to smoke cigarettes at Magoffin Institute. We didn't have what we call "ready rolls"; we rolled our own with Bull Durham or Prince Albert tobacco. I preferred Prince Albert in a can. I always called my smokes "camel" because I could not roll them straight; they always had a hump in the middle.

About 300 yards from the school was a family-owned store that sold us tobacco or anything else we needed. One time the store caught fire, and the students helped fight it by filling buckets with water from a small stream nearby. One of the problems was the ammo they sold started exploding, and that made things a little exciting. We did not save the store, but we saved the nearby house with minimal damage. What a waste; all that tobacco up in smoke! We did not always have enough money to buy cans of tobacco, which wore holes in our hip pockets. Therefore, we saved our cigarette butts and laid them on the windowsill in the dorm. We used them when we ran out of tobacco.

I learned how not to spell at Magoffin Institute. Lee, my wife, has to do all my spelling for me because I always slept during English class, which was just before lunch. And sometimes I slept through lunch. One day the teacher asked me how to spell "Mississippi." I said, "The river or the state?" Now this teacher was almost completely bald. She would swirl the side of her hair up and over the top. We were mean and sang a jingle about her but not in her presence. "On top of old baldy, all covered with skin, you might find a few hairs, but they'll be awful thin." My payback, look at me now!

One teacher, Mr. Blanton, took me under his wing and tried to keep me straight. He really loved the kids, as did the other teachers; but he went out of his way for me. One Saturday he took me to Salyersville. They were remodeling the Salyersville jail at the time and had an iron cage set up in the street to house the prisoners. All at once a gunfight broke out, and Mr. Blanton grabbed me and threw me behind a building. We got out of town soon after that.

There were lots of good things and some bad things that happened at Magoffin Institute. One night four boys held me down and rubbed salt and pepper in my eyes. When they turned me loose, I could hardly see; but I hit one of them as hard as I could in the face, and then I ran out the door. There was a bench outside the dean's apartment, and I sat there to cry and clear my eyes. The dean heard me and came out. He asked me what was wrong. After I told him, he went back in his apartment and shut the door.

I had several fights while there and won most of them. A judge sent an eighteen-year-old boy to the school from Louisville, Kentucky. I don't know what his problem was, but he ended up with a 38 revolver. Now let me tell you that I know prayer works because I am still here. He pointed that gun at my head and told me to get down and pray. Well, I did just what he said, and the prayer really worked. Later I found him and his little pimp boy without his gun. I had a little Blue Horse knife (you old people will know what I'm talking about). I pulled that knife on him, but he did not need to pray because an eighteen-year-old stocky boy is stronger than a thirteen-year-old lad. He took that knife away from me after I had nicked his wrist a little bit. He took it to his room, laid it against the baseboard, and broke both blades out of it. At least that's what his pimp told me, so I just used it as a screwdriver.

The principal at Magoffin Institute was 6'4" and all man. A few days after my incident, the guy who had the gun (Satchmo they called him) was in the middle of the gravel road with a large stick raised to hit the principal. The principal reached up, grabbed the stick, turned him around, and kicked him in the rear. That was the last we saw of Satchmo.

I believe Mama Brown's prayers worked. One night we were playing in the woods, and I didn't know there was a cliff about fifty feet high nearby. As I ran down the hill in the dark, I slammed into a tree and stopped about fifteen feet from the cliff. Thank you, Mama and Daddy Brown, for your prayers.

There were other close calls I will talk about later that my three angels protected me from. They are still with me all the time, and I even know their names. They are Surely, Goodness, and Mercy; and they will follow me all the days of my life.

My grades at Magoffin Institute were not up to par academically, so they expelled me after about a year and a half.

The next school I attended was Riverside at Lost Creek, Kentucky, in Breathitt County (also known as Bloody Breathitt). At this school I also had a guardian angel by the name of Kenneth Martin. Mr. Martin was a teacher from Wooster, Ohio, who also served as the boys' dean. He was about twenty-five years old and unmarried. He lived in the dorm with us boys. Mr. Martin loved me from the start--even when I fell in love with a girl about five years older than I. He worked hard to steer me away from her.

I think I made somewhat better grades at Riverside because the staff was a little more attentive to my needs. We also were required to learn and quote a Bible verse every day. I tried to learn a couple of weeks' worth and recited them all at once. Then I was okay for a couple of weeks. I played basketball and was in a tumbling class. Thirteen boys would kneel on their hands and knees, and I could dive over them and go into a forward roll.

Our agriculture teacher, Mr. Ellis, was an old man sixty-four years of age (sorry if it offends you sixty-four-year-olds to be called old). He taught me how not to write. He wrote things on the board and erased them before I could copy them all down. I could not write fast enough. At the age of sixty-four, he had been driving about two years and never drove over 25 mph. He owned a '55 Chevy. On this model, if you didn't lock the key into position before removing it, you could still turn the ignition switch and start the car. It just so happened that the staff was having a prayer meeting one night when Donald Johnson, one of my foster brothers from the Children's Home, and I decided to take a little ride. Donald got under the wheel, and we headed down the dirt road right past the school with big windows. Mr. Ellis just happened to be looking out and saw his vehicle going by. What would you do? Yes, he jumped up and ran after his car. We drove down the road about half a mile and came back without incident, but we were in trouble for some time. We were the talk of the school, also.

One man at Riverside helped us do work around the school. We used to shock fodder (corn stalks) and do other things around the campus. He reminded me of my dad and was about the same age and build. I loved working with him. He taught me so much. There was a water well on the campus, and one day he and I were working in the small building about five-feet square standing in a couple inches of water. As I took a rest, I leaned against the wall and stuck my fingers in a fuse box with 240 volts. It shocked me but not badly. My angels were guarding me again.

Another man who worked there had some type of balance problem. One day officers thought he had been drinking and tried to arrest him in Jackson for being drunk. He was a wonderful Christian man and never drank. He was a bit eccentric, however. I was helping to dig a hole to put a gas tank in, and that man came up to talk with us and see what we were doing. As he was walking away, I decided to throw a dirt clod over his head and let it burst in front of him as a joke. He blew up like a dollar watch and lit into me thinking I was trying to hit him. I was not; I could have if I had wanted to do so. But he convinced the staff to expel me; and even my friend, Mr. Martin, could not help me. I was out of there.

A good thing about that was that I got to spend some time with my best friend, Edward Estes, who lived near the Children's Home. I spent a lot of time with his family at their house. His parents, Ruford and Ruby Estes, fed me many good meals; and Ruby treated me just like she did Edward. The sad part is that Edward died that year from leukemia at sixteen years of age. (As a follow-up to this information, we visited Ruby a few years ago. She asked me to install a quilt rack on one wall of her bedroom. Before we left, she gave me the most beautifully hand-pieced and hand-quilted quilt. I was overwhelmed with emotion. She could have sold it for several hundred dollars, but she wanted me, "her son," to have it. We still have it.)

Anyway, let's get back to Riverside and my relationship with Kenneth Martin. He helped me in every way he could. When school was on summer break or on holidays, he took me to Wooster, Ohio, where I met many of his friends. Ma and Pa Young lived in a place called Congress. They were older than the Martins, like grandparents, and their home was always warm and comfortable. I enjoyed going to visit there.

Mr. Martin had Retinitis Pigmentosa and could not see very well. Though I was only fifteen years old, he let me do all the driving in his '58 Ford. It had an automatic transmission; and I just scooted him over next to the door (no seat belts then), adjusted the mirrors, and worked the gas and brake. I don't know why he trusted me so much, but I drove that car all over Kentucky and Ohio. We went through rainstorms and snowstorms, and I even learned how to hit a snow drift just right to slide right through it. Now, you remember my three angels? Well, they were still on duty because we never had an accident.

During summer break Mr. Martin took me to Ohio to work on a farm near Wooster. I worked there all summer for Mr. Lester who owned an eighty-acre dairy farm. He raised a lot of hay for the milk cows. He remodeled houses in town and assigned my duties each day where I worked by myself on the farm. I spread manure, raked hay, and baled hay. I loaded hay on the wagon, and at night we used an electric conveyor to move the hay to the upper floor of the barn. I also helped milk the cows and goats with electric milkers.

For some reason, his wife, Mrs. Lester, did not like me very much. One night I stayed up late to help Mr. Lester get all the hay put up. I got into bed about 2 a.m. Now, Mr. Lester always got up early and milked the cows before going to work in town. We usually ate breakfast together and then went our separate ways. One morning, I did not wake up in time; and I missed breakfast. About 8 a.m. I woke up and went downstairs, but Mrs. Lester would not feed me. I went out and worked the farm, nevertheless. That night I heard her telling Mr. Lester about it. That's when I realized that husbands and wives do not always get along or agree on some things.

I had a couple of other small incidents with his wife. Once was when I jumped on the back of one of the kid's tricycles and rode it down the sidewalk after we came home from church, but the biggest problem we had was when she drove the tractor as we baled hay. I caught the bales as they came off the baler and stacked them on the wagon about eight bales high. Yes, I learned how to do that. Mr. Lester and I unloaded them at night. Mr. Lester plowed furrows to mark his land off every six acres. Now, you can imagine what would happen to the hay stacked on a wagon if you hit those ditches with any speed at all. Mrs. Lester either did not understand--or did not care--because the first ditch loosened all the bales that I had stacked on the wagon. About seven or eight bales fell off the front. I looked at her funny but jumped off and threw a few of them back on. We took off again. Then we had a replay at the next ditch. I was beginning to get a little upset with her driving. When we arrived at the third ditch, the same thing happened. I jumped off the wagon and started walking to the house. She said, "Where are you going?" I said, "I'm going home." She said, "You come back here. You have three days before you leave, and you are going to stick it out." I stood there thinking for a while. Then I got back on the wagon, and we went to the barn. That night when she told her husband about it, there was a re-run of the breakfast incident. You would think she would learn.

I loved Mr. Lester. He was a good man and reminded me of the actor, Chuck Connors. I worked all summer for $15 a week. He put $10 in the bank for me and gave me $5. At the end of the summer, he gave me a $35 bonus. I had over $200 to take back to school. That was the most money I had ever had in my life.

There was an eighty-acre dairy farm next door to Mr. Lester, and he told me that if I would stay with him until I graduated from high school, he would buy it and give it to me. But I had to get away from that woman, and so I went back to school in Kentucky. Little did I know that I was following God's plan for my life.

In August, 1962, I enrolled at Annville Institute in Annville, Kentucky, in Jackson County. The school was a mission school run by the Reformed Church of North America. Most of our teachers were missionaries from churches in Michigan, Wisconsin, and Iowa. I continued to struggle with my grades through the junior year, but I did have lots of extra things to do.

I got up at 4 a.m. every day to help milk the cows that we raised on the farm. Then we ate breakfast in the dining hall with all the other students before going to class. Also, one of my jobs was to help stoke the boiler which supplied heat for the campus.

On the farm was a barn with a large silo at the end where we stored silage to feed the cattle during winter months. It was hard work to fill this silo; but with Ott Moore, the farm manager, supervising us, it was no problem at all. We went to the field to cut the silage before loading it into the silo. We boys got in the silo and tramped it down so that it would hold more. If we had a windstorm, Mr. Moore would always say, "Head for the silo, boys. They'll never corner us there." Mr. Moore was a good teacher and had lots of patience with us regardless of what we were doing. He was a tremendous asset to Annville Institute and was highly respected by all who knew him. He was always helping and teaching us something, whether it was killing and butchering hogs or driving the tractor safely.

One day I shot a hog three times exactly how I had been taught: one inch above and between the eyes. But it did not die. It just lay there and batted his human-looking eyes at me. So, I cut its throat to let it bleed out; and it was still alive! Next, we put it on the trailer and headed to the barn. Somewhere along the way it died. Annville Institute is the only place I remember skinning hogs instead of scraping them. At the Children's Home, we heated water and scraped the hair off. Then we used the skin to make cracklings, which were so good in cornbread. And the lard was rendered and used all year for cooking.

Work detail at Annville Institute helped pay our tuition and probably was as beneficial as our classroom studies.

There were two boys per room in our boys' dorm, and the dean and his wife lived in an apartment on the first floor. Mr. Wilkins, the boys' dean, had been in the CIA before coming to the school. The stairs leading to the upper floor were always squeaky, but he always managed to get up and down without making a sound. We tried every way to get them not to squeak for us but were never successful. I still ponder on that.

He knew everything we did and when and where we did it. The reason I know this is because one time he told us who smoked and the hiding places we used. He was very intelligent about a lot of things. I would look up words in the dictionary and ask him the meanings. He usually told us to go look it up, but sometimes he told us the answer.

I also played basketball on the Annville Bull Dogs team for Coach Jerry Hacker. Our colors were blue and orange. (A note about Coach Hacker: He was a local boy born and raised in the area. When he and his wife Alma graduated from college, they came to Annville to teach and never left. He spent his entire life in ministry to all of us at Annville. He probably never knew the impact he had on all our lives.)

I belonged to the "Stick Dance Club." We used sticks about three feet long to keep rhythm by tapping them together as we faced each other. Then we hit them on the floor. Coach Hacker was not happy at all when the new wooden floor in the gym began to get dents from the wooden poles; therefore, we moved this activity outside. This outside area beside the gym was poured concrete, and we called it "the slab." We did folk games there on Saturday nights, and it was so much fun just bonding with everyone.

I also was a pitcher on the softball team. I had a wind-up fast pitch and did very well until I struck out the coach!

I was on the pole vault team and vaulted 13.5 feet, which was good for high school. The hard work I did on the farm and at the other schools made my shoulders strong. This was a big help with pole vaulting. Mr. Doeden wanted to take me to the state competition, but we never got the opportunity. We used an aluminum pole with an aluminum triangle bar to vault over. We landed in shavings that were hauled in from the sawmill. One time my nose caught on the cross bar, and the bar came down bouncing off my head.

In shop class, one of our big projects was building a complete house for Mr. Ott Moore, the farm manager. The house we built that year is still standing in 2022.

I met a girl at that school who was my first heartthrob. Pat was not very serious about me, however. Another guy came along and stole her from me right away. Roger still brags about it. Way to go, Bro! God had a special purpose for all of us. Roger and Pat are still an awesome couple working for God all their married lives.

Remember that we talked about my guardian angels. Well, they were with me all the time at Annville except when I cut off a piece of my index finger on a lathe (a plane that smooths the wood) in shop class. That's when I got educated on what not to do when using a lathe. I lost most of my nail and about a quarter inch of the bone. Dr. Rypstra sewed it up, and I was good to go. But I thought my girlfriend, Lee, would never want to see me again.

My senior year at Annville started out with a new boys' dean. Mr. and Mrs. Jergens lived in the dorm apartment where Mr. Wilkins had lived. They were a beautiful young couple. She had been selected the Queen of Hope College in Michigan. She was our English teacher, and English was truly my worst subject. She was a nice lady and a good teacher, but she just did not understand us country kids. The first six weeks she taught Shakespeare's *Macbeth,* which I don't understand to this day. The next six weeks we did sentence diagramming which made sense to me. Then the final six weeks we did *Macbeth* again. I really tried and still could not make the grade.

Another story about Mrs. Jergens is that J. E. Hays, one of the boys in the class, was very athletic and one of our basketball stars. Now, this classroom was on the second floor with a window you could climb through. One day J. E. climbed out there and stood on the anchor that held the American flag. As Mrs. Jergens came into the classroom, J. E. climbed back through the window. She called him to the front of the classroom, and he stood looking down at her as she gave him a good dressing down! The class could not believe what we saw next. Without saying a word, he reached up and flipped the little curl hanging down on her forehead. If looks could kill, then there would have been a homicide right there. It was only two weeks till the end of school, and J. E. sat in the hallway the remainder of the year. He took his final exams in the hallway outside the classroom. J. E. later became a very successful businessman after serving in the Air Force.

I had to take two English classes my senior year to graduate. But this time I had an "Ace in the Hole," and her name was Elsa Lee Morgan.

Lee and I spent a lot of time together; I even joined the choir, and we sang together. We had a great time singing, and the school took us on "Choir Tours" up north to perform at the churches that supported the school. It was a lot of fun for us to meet them, and they loved meeting us. We laughed, and they tried to entertain us all night every night. They loved our mountain accents and how we talked. Some of their kids were quite wild when we went out to participate in activities with them. The families in the churches divided us up, and each family took three or four of us home with them to spend the night. The next morning, we rode the bus to another city. The families prepared sack lunches for the bus trip. We learned that Northerners don't know what mayonnaise is. Did you ever eat a ham sandwich with butter? This is the truth with my hand up!

Sometimes groups from the churches came to visit our school at Annville, and we took them on tours of the campus. We had fun because most of them were city folk, and we told them all kinds of things like the brown cows give chocolate milk. We told them that you make buttermilk by rolling the cow down the hill. I'm sure they didn't believe us, but they enjoyed hearing it as much as we enjoyed telling it.

The pretty brunette girl named Lee fell in love with this little orphan boy who made poor grades. Now, she was a straight-A student, so it stood to reason she had to help me with my studies if I was going to amount to anything. She was also a member of the National Honor Society and won the "I Dare You" Dale Carnegie Award. The school had a Best Christian Award--and you guessed it--she got that one, too. I can't forget the Music Award and the Best All Around Student Award. I was so blessed to be loved by her.

Now, every student who ever attended Annville Institute knows what the "Pearly Gates" were. It is an imaginary gate on the sidewalk approaching the girls' dorm. Boys were never allowed to go beyond those gates which were posts on each side of the sidewalk where a gate had once been. The girls' dean, Ms. Phelps, had eagle eyes and watched carefully all the time to see if one of the guys would "step over the line." She took her job seriously and was super protective of the girls.

Lee lived on a farm about five miles from the school. She drove her family's '56 Chevy to school in her junior year, but she stayed on campus her senior year. That meant we got to spend more time together. There were some very large trees on campus. Lee and I were very skinny at the time, but somebody in authority said we were standing too close together behind one of the trees. The school was very strict about this kind of thing, and they gave us three demerits each and sent us home for three days. If I had known what was going to happen next, I probably would have stood closer more often. Lee's mother came to school and took us both to her house for that period of expulsion. They kept me all weekend, and we went back to school as usual on Sunday after church. I never knew if Daddy Brown had been notified of the event.

Elmer and Ethel, Lee's parents, loved me from then on and treated me as part of their family. I slept in the room with Lee's young brothers, Junior and Jim. I was like a big brother to them. Occasionally, I spent weekends with them and helped Elmer bale hay and work on the farm. To be a small man, he worked very hard; and I could barely keep up with him. After work he gave me money to take Lee on a date. She had to do the driving because I did not have a license at the time. One time I carried a watermelon into the house and accidentally dropped it. It burst, and I was so embarrassed. It didn't bother her dad at all. He cut it up, and we ate it.

The Browns at the Children's Home did not have much money; and the last year I was at Annville, my senior year, they told me I was on my own. That year my brother Johnny and stepmother Annie paid my tuition for which I have always been grateful.

My angels were probably tired from working overtime to protect me while I was in the '57 Chevy with Bill House going around curves sideways, at Bond going over 100 mph, or racing through Annville with Cecil Hoskins in his Studebaker Hawk which was equipped with a sway bar which was beneficial in taking curves at high speed. I was too afraid to look at the speedometer. The road sloped down, and you could only see about 150 yards ahead. There was nowhere to go if we met another car. Thank you, Angels. God had a plan for my life.

There were only eighteen students in our May, 1964, graduating class at Annville Institute. As far as I know, most of us have done quite well.

Lee and I graduated with Paul McCowan, who was a very talented artist. I loved watching him draw, and things just began to take shape in front of my eyes. He did a pencil drawing from a portrait of Lee, and I still have it today and cherish it. I thought he surely would be a famous artist someday, and perhaps he is. After Art School in Cincinnati, Ohio, he joined the Army and became a Green Beret. It was in Airborne in Germany that he acquired a love for parachuting. When he was discharged from the Army, he continued jumping for his own pleasure. He eventually started a business and had a jump exhibition at Kings Island almost every day. He parachuted in with the American Flag near the main entrance. Lee and I went there to watch him several times. Now, he is still jumping but has expanded to include "Elvis" and takes his event all over the world. You can find his website as Paul McCowan Air Shows. His family is involved in the business with him.

Jim McWhorter married his Annville Institute soul mate, Irene Hundley. They are still married today. He became a Kentucky State Trooper and farmer among other things. He has told me about some of his experiences, and I was with him on some of them. I rode with him in the cruiser chasing bad guys, and I was with him in a boat on Lake Cumberland dealing with lawbreakers. That is, if the boat had not floated away from us. You see, we were standing on the bank talking to some people; and our boat just decided to float away. I knew Jim couldn't go after it because he was in uniform. So, guess who went after the boat. That's right, it was I. Another time we were checking someone into jail, and we saw a house on fire. When we got to the house, a little elderly woman was coming out. She had put the flames out with her fire extinguisher. Another time we were visiting, and Jim got a call to come to investigate a possible drug overdose. When we got to the house, the man was deceased. I helped Jim and the coroner place the body in a bag for transport. On one occasion,

Jim and I were on a country road where a crowd of teenagers had gathered to have a party at a local drive-in restaurant. They had built a fire in the parking lot, and there was alcohol involved, of course. Jim told them to leave, but they wouldn't listen. He opened the trunk of his cruiser, got out a camera, and started flashing pictures of them. They started scattering fast. When he got back in the cruiser, we laughed and laughed because there was no film in the camera. House fires and shootings! Now that I think about it, I should have stayed away from that guy!

Jim eventually became Chief Deputy for Pulaski County Sheriff Catron.

After graduation, Lee and I headed out into the world and went our separate ways for a spell. She went to Lexington Beauty College in Lexington and worked as a nurse's aide at Saint Joseph Hospital at night and on weekends. Some nights or weekends when she wasn't scheduled at the hospital, she worked as a waitress at the Walgreens diner on Main Street.

Life at Annville Institute was always exciting; some of the best memories of our lives. We may not have said it then, but we had a wonderful life at Annville Institute. Our teachers loved and cared for us, and I am sure there is a special place in Heaven for all of them. And we loved our staff and the students. We were like a big family. We can't think of one student or staff who intimidated or bullied any other student. I heard that in later years that may not have been the case before the school shut down in 1978. The campus became Jackson County Ministries and has hosted many elementary and middle school summer programs and remains in ministry to the community and other outreach endeavors. The campus is being upgraded; and the old school building, Lincoln Hall, is being renovated to be used for community events. Annville Institute has always had a large impact on the Annville community.

Lee and I are still connected to Annville through the Annville Institute Alumni Association. We have served as president and secretary. Also, we have helped with special projects from time to time. We love Annville and will always retain a space in our hearts for that special place.

When I was at Annville, I learned a story that I have never forgotten. It's called "Larpin' Tarpin' Coon Skin Hunting." It goes like this:

Me and my Pa lived down on Old Tar River. One day I went up and told my Pa that we should go larpin' tarpin' coonskin hunting. He said he didn't care whether we did or not. So, we went out and rounded up all the dogs but old Louse, course we rounded him up, too. And we lit out, we went down where the creek crossed the river on a foot log and started up the bank. All at once we heard the dogs treed and went around there and sure enough, right up in the top of a big sycamore sapling pine tree sat a larpin' tarpin' coonskin. I told my Pa hadn't I better go up and shake him out. He said he didn't care whether I did or not. So, I lit out and climbed about thirty or forty feet above the top of that tree. I climbed out on a rotten limb and began to shake. All at once I heard something hit the ground. I looked around. I happened to think, it might be me! All them dogs piled right on top of me. I told my Pa that I'd better knock them off, and he said he didn't care if I did or not. So, I grabbed me a big rotten club and began to beat them off. I knocked them all off but old Louse, course I knocked him off too. I told my Pa hadn't I better go around and see my Ma as we go back. He said he didn't care if we did or not. So, we went around there, and she lived in a little red house painted pink and had the windows shut wide open. I walked up to the front door as she stood there in her apron tails and said, "Come right in." I went in and spit in the bed, throwed my hat in the fire, and set right down beside her; her in one corner and me in the other. Real close you know. Well, she talked about herself, and I talked about myself until we got tired. Finally, she asked me hadn't I better go out and pick some apricots off that plum tree for her. And I said I didn't care if I did or not. Well, I went out there and climbed that old apricot tree and started shaking them plums for all I was worth. All at once I fell and landed right straddle the barbed wire fence with both legs on the same side. I told my Ma that I should go to the doctor. She said she didn't care whether I did or not. So, I saddled up old Bill and went on to the doctor. As I was coming back, I thought it would be a smart idea to go through the punkin' patch. Now, you know how the road comes around the hill there, so I just dropped down into the punkin' patch. And I looked down and there was all those punkins eating up them poor little pigs so I just reached down in my pocket and pulled out a tail and cut off the knife. Now, about that time a flock of birddogs flew over and I got out and left.

PART 3

United States Marine Corps

Parris Island, South Carolina

Camp Geiger, North Carolina

Camp Lejeune, North Carolina

Dominican Republic

Okinawa

Vietnam

JULY 1965

THE
Brown
Bagger

Joe Schaller

Transportation into the Hot Zone. 19 Operations Five were into the DMZ.

Wilbur 2017

Memorial Day 2017
Camp Nelson, Kentucky
Veterans Cemetery

2020

After graduation in 1964, I entered an unknown world. I went to Dayton, Ohio, to work with my brother Bobby hanging aluminum siding. This was a very valuable part of my training because later I got a special commendation from the Marines by using this skill at Camp Lejeune, North Carolina.

Speaking of Marines, on September 2, 1964, I joined the USMC. No, that does not stand for Uncle Sam's Misguided Children, though one time one of our rockets was misguided when it broke loose from the end of the rope. The last we saw of it was when it was headed toward the camp general's headquarters. It must have missed because we never heard any more about it.

Lee and I were dating at the time. Her dad was a WWII veteran, so he was very proud of me.

I went through basic training at Parris Island, South Carolina. Basic training is an experience you can get no place else. The DI (Drill Instructor) hit me in the stomach with a helmet liner called a "chrome-dome," and this was the start of my training. My Platoon Number was 280, and we were housed on Panama Street. We Marines learned that you have to work as a team; and if one person made a mistake, we all had to pay. This encouraged us to help each other and pull together. We picked up large logs and carried them around to enforce this training. We fought each other with padded pogo sticks to teach us how to fight. We learned to use a bayonet on the end of an M1 rifle doing the slash, vertical butt stroke, jab, and smash with the butt of the gun.

We crawled beside sandbags with quarter-pound TNT exploding on the other side while machine guns fired live ammunition over our heads. We learned to cross triple-strand, double-strand, and single-strand ropes without falling. We had classes during the day and took notes in a notebook that we had to have in front of our faces studying anytime we were standing still. We had to memorize a lot of information about the Marines and the United States Government.

Two weeks before graduation, the DI did not even know my name because I tried to keep a low profile. We always stood at ease at the foot of our bunk beds at mail call. The DI stood in the middle of the squad bay and called out names. When or if your name was called, you would run up to face him and receive your mail. My bunk was about

45 degrees from the DI. When he gave one guy his mail, the DI made a joke about all the letters the guy received. When the guy did an "about face" to return to his bunk, he laughed out loud. That was a no-no. Well, I smiled because I couldn't believe this guy just laughed out loud in front of the DI. And wouldn't you know it, the DI was looking right at me. I was caught smiling! I had to do bends and thrusts till bedtime, and the next day several people who messed up were up early to go on a forced march around the island with me! Gomer Pyle had company on this march! Goooollleee, Sarge!

While we were on this forced march, Sgt. Baker, a black man who was a Marine Corps boxing champion and a great DI, told one of the Marines to find a snake. He assumed he could never find one, but he did and brought it to the DI. Talk about a DI going crazy! At that time, I did not know a DI could run as fast backward as he can forward.

Now, if you are in boot camp and you get sick or can't swim, you are set back until you get well or learn to swim. Then you are put with another platoon so you can graduate with all the training that's required.

One enlisted recruit came to our platoon though he was a college professor. He said he wanted to see what the Corps was like from the bottom up. When Sgt. Baker came to us, we could not understand him very well. This college professor couldn't understand him either. This was sad and funny, too. When the DI called cadence, this Marine could not understand him. The platoon was going in one direction, and this recruit was going in the other. A lot of the time the DIs acted like they were mad; but in this case, I believe Sgt. Baker really did get mad. He not only threw his Smokey Bear hat (cover) down, but he jumped on it. Then he made the Marine climb into the nearby dumpster. Now, when they let us smoke, we stood in a circle with a bucket of water in the middle of the circle where we extinguished our cigarette butts. When we were finished smoking, the bucket would be dumped into the dumpster. The DI ordered the men to dump the bucket on top of the Marine who was still in the dumpster. I really felt bad for this guy, but he did fine after that and graduated with us.

Most of our DIs really wanted us to succeed and become good Marines, but we had one who did things to us for his pleasure. He seemed to get pleasure out of torturing the recruits. He was gone in about two weeks. I think Sgt. Hill, our Senior DI, saw to it. We did not know that Staff Sgt. Hill was a Methodist preacher, but he was not with us a lot of Sundays. He explained this to us the night before graduation.

On the rifle range, we practiced a lot of snapping in and shooting in order to get a good score on graduation day. Snapping in is where you sit in a circle around a barrel and aim at targets painted on the barrel. One Marine always shot what we called an "unk" score (not qualified), and he was told that if he did not qualify on graduation day, he had better go "awol." Sure enough, they caught him running away about 500 yards from us.

This was just the beginning of our training. While we were there, we took a test to find out what field we would most likely fit into or be the best at. I don't know why, but I ended up in Combat Engineers (Military Occupation Specialty 1371). We learned a little about different kinds of bridges, cables, ropes, etc. My special field was demolitions, working with explosives and mines. I spent a lot of time with TNT and C-4 explosives.

Graduation at Parris Island was a big deal. Several parents came to see their sons and daughters graduate, and lots of pictures were taken. I did not tell Lee that she and the family could come to graduation, and they were disappointed when they found out. I did not know then that Elmer Morgan would have moved heaven or earth to be there for my graduation. I didn't see them until I had completed training at Camp Geiger.

From Parris Island we went straight to Camp Geiger in North Carolina near Camp Lejeune Marine Base on the East Coast. Camp Geiger is the Weapons Training Center. We trained on M14 rifles, M60 machine guns, mortars, rifles, pistols, and rifle grenades, which was the most powerful shoulder weapon I ever shot. We shot day and night, and the night practice was very colorful when every fifth round was a tracer.

After about a month at Geiger, we were assigned our duty stations. Mine was the 2nd Marine Division, Combat Engineers, at Camp Lejeune, North Carolina.

At Lejeune we looked forward to "Liberty" every day when our duties were done. A lot of the Marines would go to the Enlisted Club for entertainment with bands or just to unwind and drink beer. As time passed, I sat with the guys and took a sip of their beers. I began to like it but decided that this is not going to be who I am. So, one night I decided to quit. In order to do this, I decided to get really drunk. All the guys were buying me beer. I could not even see the band which was about twelve feet away. I was so silly I just laughed all the time. One of them led me to the head (bathroom) every five minutes. After nineteen Colt 45 malt liquors who would not be this way? I don't remember how I got to the barracks, but I was sick for three days and could not stand in formation. That was the last time I ever took a sip of beer. I tell people all the time that it tastes like horse pee, and I do know what horse pee tastes like. Remember Mert and Kate? They had long tails that occasionally smacked you in the face!!

I never drank after that, but I do tell people that I bought three beers one time and got drunk as a dog. Yep, I spilled one, gave one away, and drank one. That's my story and I'm sticking to it.

We were called to the Dominican Republic for a conflict that was going on. There was civil war on the island, and the Marines were trying to get a peaceful outcome. I was sent to Cherry Point, North Carolina, to fly to the Dominican Republic. I rode all the way in a personnel carrier inside a C-130 airplane. As soon as we landed, there was gunfire in our compound. It wasn't enemy fire, but a Marine who needed more training on unloading his 45-caliber pistol. Someone forgot to tell him to remove the magazine before ejecting the round out of the chamber. Otherwise, you reload another shell into the chamber. Fortunately, no one was hurt as he shot it into the ground.

The Dominican Republic is where Columbus is buried. We could see his really tall monument from our compound, but we never got to visit it since it was in enemy territory.

We soon moved up on a small hill where the Ambassador's dwelling was located, and this is where we set up camp. The Ambassador had a swimming pool with a fence around it. Now, you know that a fence has never meant a lot to a Marine with a "can-do" attitude because we had been taught how to breach them. One morning about 2 a.m. I awoke to someone yelling. When I went to see, I thought I was dreaming. There was our Major with about twenty of our Marine engineers standing at attention around the pool without one stitch of clothing.

This was funny to those of us who were not involved, but I think I had a nightmare after that. I'm not sure what price the Major made them pay, but I'm sure they will never forget it. I would love to hear this story from one of them. I wonder how long they stood at attention while being "dressed down" by the Major. Oh, wait; they were already dressed down!

We were not there long before the local girls began visiting the compound, especially at night. We were blessed with a three-seater portable toilet, and there I sat one afternoon when a girl walked in and sat down right beside me. She did her thing and got up and walked out. I was in shock. I don't remember if I did what I went in there for or not. Today, in 2022, I'm sure that would be perfectly normal in some places.

One of our engineers got captured by the enemy, but within a few hours he escaped and was back to our compound with a hair-raising story.

As engineers, we were called to deal with explosives or just to check things out. I never did a lot of gun-fighting, but I did have some experiences there that I never had before. One was my first earthquake, which made the ground and trees shake pretty good.

One day we walked down the street following some tank tracks. We were surprised when the tracks veered off to the side of the street. One track ran right up the back of a parked car and right back down the front leaving that car almost flat and destroyed. I guess somebody was not happy about being there and wanted to leave a message.

When I was in Vietnam, I was shot at from a lot of directions but never from the sky because America owned the skies over Vietnam. The first and only time I was shot at from the sky was when I was in the Dominican Republic. It was a bright sunny day, and some of us engineers were in the street building roadblocks to direct traffic and tanks. Ha! Suddenly, I heard the engine of an airplane change sound because it was going into a dive. I looked up and saw it coming down toward us. Then bullets started bouncing off the pavement around us. I saw the muzzle flashes from the guns on the plane. It didn't take me long to forget about roadblocks and hammers. I ran into an unfinished house and got into a corner with my head against the wall. This plane made one pass and was gone. I found out later that one of our engineers from our campsite at the Ambassador's Compound picked up his M-60 machine gun and shot several rounds at the plane. I don't think he hit it, but this gun is powerful enough to bring that plane down.

We were in the Dominican Republic for thirty-six days in May and June, 1965, and then we came back to Camp Lejeune.

Shortly after returning to Camp Lejeune, Lee, my high school girlfriend, called to say we were going to get married. My story is that I said, "But we have no money." She said, "If we wait until we have money, we will never get married." That is not the way she remembered it. Her story is that before I left, I had told her to make wedding plans and give me at least a one-month notice to get approval for leave. So, what could I say? And with my Captain's blessing on August 2, 1965, we were married in her parents' house on Sunrise Hill in Jackson County, Kentucky.

I took her back to Camp Lejeune. Now that there were two of us, we had to find housing. Camp Knox, just off the main base, was military housing with tiny silver campers. Who cares, we wanted to be close anyhow. These trailers were silver outside and about twenty feet long. It was really cozy, especially in August in hot North Carolina. We left both doors and all the windows open to get some air circulating.

Married Marines were called "brown baggers" because they took their lunch in brown bags instead of standing in chow line. One of our friends was an artist, and he drew the funniest sketch and named it the "brown bagger."

Our daughter, Connie, was born at the Camp LeJeune Naval Hospital on July 24, 1966. While she was being delivered, I watched *Bonanza* downstairs. We had moved to a larger trailer at this time, and the baby bed was on the wall over the head of our bed! Not a bad setup.

We were rich back then. Lee received $70 per month, and I got about $80. We were just as happy as we could be. Lee borrowed $1,000 from her grandfather to buy the cutest green Buick Skylark. We drove it on several trips back to Kentucky. Eventually we sold it and bought a little red Opal Cadet. It was a small car, and we drove to the drive-in theatre on base. As we drove over the humps looking for a parking space, one guy yelled for me to "lower the blade; it ain't cutting the grass!"

Lee thoroughly loved military life. She was active in our church there and got acquainted with a lot of the other military wives. They joined the clubs together, did laundry together, knew what each other was making for dinner, whose husbands were on bivouac, and who was expecting and when. They watched out for each other; family away from home.

Training every day was a part of our lives at Camp Lejeune. We set mines on Onslow Beach for the War College to come down and observe what looked like a plane strafing as we exploded our charges lined up on the beach. While this was going on, our Amtrac (assault amphibian vehicle) fleet made a beach landing with troops pouring out of the AmTracs to swarm the beaches. Sometimes I was in the landing team, and other times I was with the team exploding charges on the beaches. Families were invited to attend this event. Lee came down to the beach and sat in the bleachers with all the other families and invited dignitaries.

I once was assigned to an Amtrac. It was called a LVTE1 (Landing Vehicle, Tracked, Engineer, Mark 1) because it was manned by engineers who could operate the explosives on board. It had a one-inch nylon line surrounded by C-4. It was about 100 yards long with a rocket at the front end to pull it out of the bin where it was attached and lay it through a mine field to explode and breach a path. AmTracs traveled on land and in water and are launched from a LST (Landing Ship Tank). This is what we practiced at our Onslow Beach landings.

I had a lot of exciting training experiences as a Marine. One of them was disembarking from a ship by climbing down a mesh rope to a landing craft known as a LVT (Landing Vehicle Transport). This is very dangerous in many ways. You had to make sure you were wearing your helmet with the strap pulled tight because often someone would drop his rifle on the men below. Not only was it difficult to climb down with all your gear, but getting off the rope into the small boat waiting below was something that required training. The little boat below is bobbing up and down in a different rhythm than the one you are leaving. If you stepped off the rope when the boat below was going down, you could fall ten-twelve feet into the boat. One thing that helped was that the first two men down the rope would station themselves on either side of the rope and hold it tight and tell you when to step off. This was important practice because when we got to Vietnam this is the procedure that some Marines used to disembark to go inland. I disembarked via helicopters.

Part of Marine training is going on a six-month Mediterranean or a three-month Vieques Island cruise to practice making these landings. After the Dominican conflict, we went on a Vieques Island cruise. Vieques Island is where we did our training, and our liberty call was to San Juan, Puerto Rico. I went to the San Jeronimo Hilton Casino where I always ordered milk with ice in it. When I got back to the States, I always drank iced milk. I still do on occasion.

While on the cruise, our orders were to stand by because trouble had started up again on the Dominican Republic. We extended our cruise and floated in squares waiting for word to deploy. We thought we would be making a beach landing since we were on a LST (Landing Ship Tank) that carried AmTracs in its belly. So, we floated around for several days offshore; and our food supply ran low before we could get replenished. We ate baked beans a couple times a day. This didn't last long, but other ships tried to stay away from us!!! I guess there was some kind of cloud that was following us. It was scary to think they might stop all smoking on the ship and extinguish our smoking lamps.

Now the Vietnam War was getting lots of attention, and it was obvious that I would be going at some point. Connie was about four months old when I got my orders in November, 1966. I took my thirty-day leave before reporting to Camp Pendleton Marine Corps Base in California. I checked in on January 1, 1967, for jungle training to prepare for Vietnam. We learned how to survive. We learned how to escape and evade from prison, how to live off the land, watch the monkey, eat what he eats, then eat the monkey. We learned making and avoiding booby traps of all kinds.

After about a month of training we boarded a ship called the USS Lindenwald which had been an ice breaker in Alaska. Several hundred of us were headed for Vietnam. Some of the Marines and sailors were musicians. A band was put together, and they played on deck each day for us. One of the Marines was a professional. Perhaps you remember the song "Wild Weekend" by The Rebels in 1963. It didn't have words, just music; and the guy who wrote it played it live for us on his saxophone. We loved it. It was really popular at that time. Also, they played "Wipe Out" by the Surfaris in 1963.

I did not know this then, but Okinawa is on the route to Vietnam. Orders came down that 300 Marines would be getting off at Okinawa instead of going to Vietnam. My three angels again--I was one whose name was on that list.

Camp Hanson, Okinawa, was my new home where I was assigned to be an instructor at a "Jungle Lane" where we trained Marines who were headed to Vietnam. At this camp we taught Marines how to cross one-, two-, and three-strand ropes. We taught them how to recognize and avoid booby traps and mines. There were several instructors who had already been to Vietnam, and they taught me a lot of things that I believe helped me survive the war. These were things that I didn't have to learn with my life when they happened. I was prepared. Again, I believe that this was my angels protecting me.

"Jungle Lane" was up in the mountains on the northern part of the island. Every day we took our C-rations and drove up there for the classes. We often gave our rations to an Okinawa native who lived there. Then he fed us strange native foods, like whale blubber, in his hut. He got a pension every month from our government because he helped us take the island in WWII. He had a spider monkey with a long tail. It was very friendly and climbed all over us while stealing our cigarettes, ink pens, or anything else we had in our pockets. If you wanted to see a monkey go crazy, just try to get the item back. The old man was the only one who could get it for you.

We did not have a class every day, so our "Gunny" (Gunnery Sgt.) took us driving around the island where we got to see a lot of interesting things and places. On some days off, we played with our props. One of them was shotgun shells with only powder in them that we used for our booby traps. We took this powder out and tried to make a rocket with bamboo and a fuse. From the launching pad, these homemade rockets chased us around the property and the building where we kept our supplies. It is amazing that we didn't blow up the island.

We also had a cable that ran down the side of the mountain for about 100 yards from a platform to a pond at the base. I figured we went about 50 mph down this thing. You held onto two ropes as the wheel rolled down the cable. A trainer stood down below to tell you when to let go so that you landed in the water. You are going so fast you must turn loose over land so as to hit the water. If your timing was wrong, you hit a rope net at the end of the cable. I never did have to go down this thing, nor did I want to.

After a couple of months our Gunny came to me and asked if I wanted to join his men. He was putting together a Battalion Landing Team on the ship USS Okinawa. I was a Sgt. E5 at this time, and I told him it was okay with me. We started preparing to go to war.

After boarding the ship, we headed for Vietnam where my first of nineteen operations started on April 27, 1967. This operation was called "Operation Beaver Cage." As we prepared on the night before this first operation, some of our engineers were transferred to one of our other ships. As they loaded onto the CH-34 helicopter, the last man to get on board was a Hispanic sergeant who was a hero in our book. The chopper lost its lift for some reason and went off the side of the ship. Since the sergeant was the last one to get on, he did not have a seat belt and was just in the door when it crashed. The two pilots and another engineer got out alive. The engineer that survived tried to come up out of the water, and the propeller blades hit him on the helmet. He went back under and swam away from it. This really messed him up, and they had to keep an eye on him for a while. The reason I say the sergeant was a hero is because the Marine who survived told me that the sergeant tried to get some of the men out of their seatbelts, and he gave his life because of it. The greatest love is to lay down your life for a friend. The next day our war began as we were still dealing with our loss.

On our ship, the USS Okinawa, the hospital and morgue were at opposite ends of the ship. The ship had an elevator on each side of the ship to move the choppers from the hanger deck (inside the ship) to the flight deck. The hanger deck is where we prepared our weapons and loaded our magazines the night before an operation. The day of the operation we were placed into what is called a "hilo" team, and we lined up to load onto the helicopters to be transported to the area of battle for that operation. If there were people hurt or wounded in battle, they brought them back to the ship where they went either to the medical area or to the morgue. Remember, these two areas were on opposite ends of the ship, and you watched which end of the ship the helicopter that you are about to board went to. You can imagine how this could affect you as you are heading out to the area they just came from. The ship's loudspeakers announced which elevator will be used – starboard (the hospital) or port (the morgue).

Sometimes on an "operation" there was no resistance from the enemy during landing and everything went okay. However, if we met resistance, we went to Plan B, which was an alternate "LZ" if the landing zone was too "hot." In some cases, the "LZ" was too hot, but some Marines had already disembarked. We had to develop another plan to evacuate them or bring in more forces. Being an engineer, I was never in the first wave into the landing zone but was sometimes in the second wave.

We were usually a driving force or a blocking force to stop and trap the enemy. Most of our operations were anywhere from about ten miles south of Da Nang to the upper side of the DMZ (Demilitarized Zone). My orders said I was detached from Dung Ha, but I was only there for three days; and we got mortared every day. This was the most northern Marine Outpost in Vietnam. I was glad to get back on ship.

We were on ship after returning from another operation when we were sent back out to help Battalion 1/9 who had gone into the DMZ and had been overwhelmed by the Viet Cong. I think there were 35,000 NVA (North Vietnamese Army) just north of the DMZ, and they were walking south under their own mortars and rockets and were stabbing our men who had their heads down in the foxholes. We landed south of the DMZ and walked three miles north to help BTN 1/9 while all the time we had to take cover from mortars and sniper fire. As an engineer, I was usually close to the command post and was seldom up on the front lines; but this time two 60 mm mortar men and I were digging a foxhole basically in sandy soil. I was in the hole and had dug it about twenty inches deep. I got out to let one of them dig; and while I was squatting on the edge watching him, rockets started coming in and bouncing off the trees all around us. Instantly I heard "Corpsman up!", which are the words you hate to hear in combat. But if you are one of those in need, I guarantee you that our Navy corpsmen will literally go through hell to get to you. I don't know where the Navy gets these guys, but they are my heroes.

For those of you who have never experienced this, when a rocket is fired, you can't hear it till it is right on your head and you hear a little swish sound. Mortars are different because you can hear them come out of the tube several hundred yards away, and you hear them as they come down in your area. It was just whether it was your time or not, if you know what I mean. Anyhow, as this mortar got closer and closer and the whistle got louder and louder, I just knew it had my number on it; and I dived in that hole so fast I did not even get my hands in front of my face and almost choked to death on the sand and dirt. Those mortar men went to set their mortars up somewhere, and I never saw them again. It was so bad there that I lay in that hole for two days. The mortars were so close that shrapnel went down my collar and burned my neck.

This was one of the few times we had motorized vehicles with us. We had tanks with a 90 mm gun on top. At one point, the enemy was shooting at us from their foxholes and had already killed several of our Marines, so we were laying low, at least I was. As the tanks came forward, it started to rain hard, and I thought the tanks were going to run over me. Some of our men got behind the tanks as they advanced. Two of the enemy poked their heads up out of their foxhole and started shooting at us, but the tank took care of them. He turned that 90 mm toward them, and the hole disappeared. We loaded several of our dead and wounded onto the tanks to be transported out of the area. Marines never leave live or dead Marines behind. Some of our government leaders need to know that. As we got to the upper side of the DMZ, what we saw was devastating because there were dead Marines everywhere. One company had only eight men left who could still fight. Our mission was to go in and get the dead and wounded out, so we loaded them onto tanks to take them south and out of the danger area. There were so many mortars and rockets coming in that the men had to crawl under the tanks till it let up. As we were leaving the area, the Major was yelling "run" as mortars were hitting right behind us. He did not have to repeat that order. Marines call this "advancing to the rear."

Speaking of foxholes, on another operation we stopped to take a rest. The Viet Cong (VC) started walking mortars in on us. To do this, they move the target up, or aim about 100 yards higher after each set of mortar rounds. I could tell they were headed straight toward us, but some of the Marines started laughing at me when I started digging a hole. It was sandy soil and easy to dig. The Marines leaned back on their packs; but as the rounds got closer, they lay flat on their backs on the ground. My head and part of my body were in the hole I had just dug. After the mortars passed, I had green paint from the entrenching tool handle all over my hands because of the sand and sweat. The next time these guys listened to me. I had the last laugh.

Sometimes strange things happened in Vietnam. One of our Marines had heat exhaustion, and another Marine carried him and his gear about 200 yards to a medevac chopper. As we watched, the Marine who was doing the carrying got on the chopper and left. The Marine being carried came back to us. I guess he was okay.

One time our company was pinned down with the Viet Cong shooting at us from both sides. It was not funny at the time, but the Gunny said they couldn't get away because "they've got us surrounded."

Once we had some wounded men, and a medevac chopper came in to get them. The chopper was shot down, but another chopper came right in behind that one and extracted them. Chopper pilots and corpsmen are my heroes. I'm glad this was not Benghazi with those so-called leaders in charge. We will die going after our fellow Marines.

Another time there was a Viet Cong up in a tree about 300 yards away shooting at us. The Major called up the 3.5 rocket launcher (a recoilless rifle). That Marine had three rockets to shoot. He shot two of them and missed, but the third one made the threat go away. It was like "poof." He's gone.

I blew up a lot of 500-pound bombs. They are about eighteen inches in diameter and seven feet long. I had never seen one with the fins still attached. The fins help to stabilize it as it falls. The fins are about eight feet across. When they hit the ground, the fins always break off if the bomb does not explode. These fins have holes in them and look a little like beach matting (metal grating for vehicle tires and treads). As

I looked down, I was standing on a set of those fins with the bomb still attached. It was buried completely in the ground at a small angle with only the fins showing. Being an engineer, I knew that a slight vibration could set that thing off, so I cleared out of that area as fast and as gently as I could. We were on the move and did not have time to deal with it at the time.

On another occasion I walked up on a round, metal plate about five inches in diameter that said "bomb fragmentation," and it had a lot number which identified it as a bomb. And only the metal plate was above ground. After I cleared the area of Marines, I took about three feet of time fuse with a quarter-pound block of C-4 and lit the fuse with an igniter. I ran over the hill. Now time fuses burn about thirty to forty-five seconds per foot, so I had about ninety seconds till explosion. I waited and waited, but there was no explosion. Now things really started getting exciting. I crawled back up to the bomb. I could see that the time fuse had stopped burning about a foot from where I had lit it. That meant it had about sixty to ninety seconds left. I cut it with my crimpers, split it with my knife, and lit it again with my cigarette. Back over the hill I scurried to wait. It never did explode, and I told the captain that I would put a hand grenade on it and run. But he said, "No"; and we moved out leaving the C-4 explosive and the bomb behind. I am so glad he did not let me use the grenade because they have a three- to five-second delay after the pin is pulled and the spoon released. I am not fast enough to outrun that. Do you think that Captain could have been one of my angels?

Another day a Marine and I went outside our perimeter to blow up some mortar rounds. A firefight broke out, and we were in the middle. We tried to be invisible. I guess we did okay because we got back inside our perimeter safely.

Our training did not teach us to wake up the captain when two choppers ran together and crashed. We were running everywhere because when something is falling from the sky, it looks like it is coming right at you. Nobody stopped to wake the captain who was napping, and one of the choppers crashed about 200 feet from him. At that moment, he was not a happy Marine to say the least. It's hard to wake the captain when you are running away as fast as you can. The tail rotor was knocked off and the chopper spun to the ground; no one was hurt severely that time. Except we thought the captain might hurt us!

Another time some of our Marines were sent to help another company that was in a big firefight. One other engineer and I were put on the perimeter line to protect the 105 howitzers that were in that location. It was late at night and very dark. So that the Marines who were in the firefight could see, flares started dropping from C-130 planes. When that happens, we were taught to stand still and close one eye so that you don't lose your night vision. Well, there I stood right out in the open. I followed protocol while looking for a place of safety when the flares stopped. It seemed they would never stop, but finally there was a break. I headed for a hole I had spotted. Now when the big guns set up, they dig a big hole in the ground to store the ammo in. You guessed it! I landed right on top of those rounds. I got my 130 pounds below the ground and just lay there and watched the planes drop the flares. I felt so safe. The only thing that would have gotten me was a direct hit, and I would have been missing in action because nothing would have been left.

A 500-pound bomb landed about 100 yards from me one time. I'm glad there was a large mound of dirt about 100 feet tall between me and it. Talk about close air support, but it was not good for the ears.

There were lots of hedgerows in Vietnam. A couple of Marines passed through a particular one before I went through a smaller opening. Just a few minutes later someone found an anti-personnel mine right where our feet should have found it. But remember, my angels were there, so I went back and blew up the mine.

Our company found ourselves in a mine field one time. On that operation, my engineers carried mine detectors and knew how to use them. But for some reason, the infantry wanted to get across this area fast. The Major kept yelling for us to quickly get a path made so the Marines could get through. Well, there was lots of shrapnel in the ground along with the mines. We used our probes to find out what each item was, and that took time. The Major's men spread out and started going around us. Every few minutes we watched as a Marine was hurt from a mine, but I kept my Marines safe and none of them was hurt. It was so scary that I wished I could get a minor injury just to get out of there. I never wanted to see another mine field. General Schwarzkopf said that when you are in a mine field, you know what intense is. Yes, I know the feeling.

Poem: "A Man Is Never Truly Dead Until He Is Forgotten" from the book *I Never Heard the Thunder* written by Jim Curtis and used with his approval:

I can't recall his given name
We always called him Doc
But I do remember all the time
The two of us would talk.

He really didn't believe in war
And said that he was scared
But when we hollered Corpsman up
I never saw that fear.

He'd risk it all to save a life
And sometimes he would cry
But only when he lost a man
Or heard a friend had died.

So here's to him
That long lost friend
That pushed aside his fear
And if we ever meet again
I'll refer to him as Sir!

A corpsman in the Navy was called "Doc," with all respect due him. When I meet a corpsman or a helicopter pilot today, I salute them out of respect because of what I have seen them do in combat. Once a corpsman in Vietnam pulled me out of a rice paddy after I had passed out because of an infection.

Speaking of rice paddies, one crazy thing about Vietnam was the water buffalos that were led and directed with a small stick or a push in the rear by the Vietnamese boys and girls. Sometimes the buffalos had rings in their noses, and the children led them that way. The strangest thing was that as soon as one of these animals saw a Marine in green, it would attack. Several times I saw this happen, and the Marine shot the animal to stop it. Otherwise, the Marine ends up with a broken back or other injury and must be evacuated. In either case, when we killed one of those buffalos or cut a piece of bamboo, the United States government had to pay the family for it. So much for war.

Battalion Landing Team 1/3 was the first battalion that went ashore in Vietnam fully equipped with M-16 rifles except for us engineers who kept our M-14s. This was a bigger gun and had a longer range. One time the Viet Cong were shooting mortars at us from about 700 yards. Another Marine, who had been on a shooting team, took one of our engineer's M-14 and killed all three of those Viet Cong.

At one point, we evacuated a lot of dead and wounded men. Because of the weight on the chopper, they left some of their gear behind to be taken out later. I thought I would carry the smaller and lighter M-16 one time, and that was the last time for that.

On the only operation I ever made on an Amtrac in Vietnam, I was about halfway back in the vehicle with thirty-five Marines. "The line of departure" is the point approximately 100 yards from shore when the order is given to "Lock and Load." This means that when the ramp comes down, we are ready to fire. Now these Tracs carry 30- or 50-caliber rifles on top. I was one scared Marine when I heard shots being fired and thought the enemy was shooting at us. But I discovered it was the vehicle beside us clearing the beach by gaining fire superiority so we could land safely. The enemy had left before we got there. Remember my three angels?

A piece of land jutted out into the ocean just a few miles north of Da Nang. The Marines had discovered a group of caves and tunnels in a mountain, and they needed our engineers to destroy them. Four engineers and I were sent about three miles away from where we were dug in. We loaded onto AmTracs. (They always sent two vehicles because they tended to get high centered, and one could push the other free.) We also had a freelance reporter with us who had also been in the Marines as a Lance Corporal. We went to the base of a hill where we were supposed to meet a man who would take us up to where we were needed. As we were advancing at the base of the hill after leaving the AmTracs, the photographer beside me said, "There is a Viet Cong." That's when I went into survival mode. As I was saying, "Where?", I was looking for a rock to hide behind. There was a cliff in front of us about fifty feet high, and that Viet Cong was standing on top of it when I saw him. Now, the problem was instead of my regular M-14 rifle, I had the M-16 rifle which I had never carried before. I knew where the safety was on the side and that you operated it with your thumb. On the M-14 you operated the safety with your index finger inside the trigger guard. Now while I was trying to sort through all this, the Viet Cong was looking down at us but was not being aggressive. One of us had to make a move, so I hollered, "Hey!" He threw his hand up and in perfect English he responded, "Hey!" I was so relieved at his response because I was getting ready to take him off that cliff. This was the man they had sent down to lead us up the hill. He was a South Vietnamese man who was on our side. I believe we both had our angels busy that day. Our shape charges had been loaded onto helicopters and transported to the top of the hill so that we did not have to pack them up there. I can't believe they did this. Something went right. A Sergeant must have made this decision.

The USS Okinawa had lots of things we needed and enjoyed. One of those things was good, cold water each time we came back onboard. One day another Marine and I were outside our perimeter destroying some dud mortar ammunition. As we came back into our perimeter, we met a Major who had just come from the ship on a chopper. He stuck his metal canteen out in front of me with ice cold water beads running down the sides and told me to drink. I said, "No, Sir; you keep it." He said, "Drink, Marine." I handed it to my partner, and he took a good big drink and handed it back to me. I tried to drink it all, but it still had a little left in it when I gave it back to the Major. The Major was happy and so were we. Marine officers are trained well and care for their men. They never eat until the men under them have been served.

On one operation a Marine had a bullet go in the front of his helmet while we were in a gunfight. The bullet went around the helmet liner and came out the back of the helmet. He was not hurt but was really shaken up. He sent that helmet home. The next day this same guy had a bullet hit the plastic piece on top of his M-14 and busted it. Again, he was not hurt. I told him I wanted to stay close to him. I don't know what his angels' names were.

We went to the Philippines when the ship had to resupply. I remember the people there being very aggressive. One day as I walked down the street, a little boy wanted to shine my boots, which were already spit shined. I refused him. When I looked down, he had put a big gob of shoe polish on the toe of my boot. He ran off so I couldn't twist his arm or kick his backside. We experienced problems with some young Filipino boys. Marines bought gifts or other things from the vendors; and as they walked down the street to go back to the ship, a young Filipino boy would jump out from a hiding place, grab the items, and run. If you chased him, he would have his buddies grab you and give you a good beating. Several of our Marines experienced this. You can understand why our Marines were angry and upset.

I talked one of our men who experienced this out of a plan he came up with to get even. His plan was to take a grenade, put it in a box with a hole in the bottom for the pin, and a ring to stick through and attach to his finger. Then when they grabbed the box, it would pull the pin and the grenade would explode in the box as the thief ran away. The box would explode in about three to five seconds. I never heard that anyone actually did this, at least I hope not.

Somehow or other I was chosen to go into Da Nang to be a casualty reporter for all our engineers that were killed or wounded. I reported this information back to the ship by radio. One night about eight of us were going around the airport in the back of a personnel carrier driven by a drunk Marine. We hit a gasoline tanker head on. No one was killed, but we were laid up for a while. I had only a few months left on my tour to Vietnam, so they sent me back to Okinawa where I was assigned to the woodworking shop.

I left there a month early and returned to the States when a message came that my father-in-law, Lee's dad, had died. That was December, 1967. We returned to Camp LeJeune for eight more months, and then I was discharged from the USMC on September 2, 1968, as a SGT E5.

There are lots more stories I could tell you, but I don't want to bore you. I was in Vietnam about seven months and did nineteen operations, five of them were in the DMZ.

While I was overseas, Lee worked with her dad at the Bluegrass Army Depot near Richmond, Kentucky.

A few times since leaving the Marines, we have returned to Parris Island and Camp Lejeune. One time we attended the graduation of a friend and other times just to revisit our old home and reminisce. At Camp Lejeune one time we were at the "Guest House" on base, and a very nice gentleman behind the desk explained that it was for family members of a Marine who was stationed there. As we talked, I explained that I had been a Marine there thirty years earlier. He said, "Sir, you are my guest tonight." He allowed us to stay there.

One occasion I distinctly remember is when I returned for a special visit to Parris Island with a group of old VFW Marines from Kentucky. The trip was interesting and memorable to say the least. We visited the PX (Post Exchange). One of the fellows used his ID pass to let me shop for a set of dress blues. I never had the money to afford them when I was in the Marines. Usually, it took several days to get the uniform tailored to fit and the stripes put on; but the tailor, who was a female, said she would rush it through since we were leaving the next day. I went into a dressing room and put on the slacks, and she had me stand on a step so she could measure the hem. Now we were on a tight schedule, and the guys were waiting for me in the van to go to dinner. She finished measuring the hem and said, "Okay, take them off now." I just unzipped them and dropped them right there in front of her. As I stood in my underwear, we both started laughing. I apologized, and she said that she had seen everything before. I dressed and quickly got out of there after giving her my phone number. About two hours later she called and said they were ready for me to pick up. As I was leaving, she handed me the paper with my phone number on it. I said that after what I had done, we were pretty tight and that she could keep it. We had another big laugh. "Life is like a box of chocolates."

PART 4

Fayette County Fire Department

Post-Vietnam Life

Fire Department

Haz-Mat

Old Fashioned Days Fire Prevention Parade

Lisa - First Lexington Female Firefighter

Santa Suits up for Hazmat class

MY CREW GAVE ME THIS AT RETIREMENT

For
OUTSTANDING PERFORMANC
on and off the field,
FIRE CAPTAIN
WILBUR WHITE
has been awarded this
"Swift and bold"
Token of our appreciation
IACPFF
1995

Kristin, Wilbur, Joe, John

Best Crew Ever!

Lexington's First Female Fire Chief, Kristin Chilton

Now this part of my life may seem mixed up by the stories that I tell. Like most firefighters, I worked various jobs while I was on the Fire Department and Sheriff's Department. And I still do, for that matter. Like I said in my disclaimer, the stories may not be chronologically correct.

I had no idea what I was going to do when I left the Marines. We came to Lexington and stayed with my dad and stepmom for about four weeks. The first day we were in Lexington I went to the old county fire station on New Circle Road near Meadow Lane. I asked them if they knew where I could find a job. One of the guys sent me to the city fire station on Third Street and told me to ask for Jim Long. I arrived in town on Friday and went to work for Jim on Monday making $3.25 per hour doing construction work and driving big trucks. A CDL was not required back then. Jim taught me how to do a lot of things and treated me like a son.

Lee and I found an apartment at 1917 Cambridge Drive. We bought all new furniture at the HH Leet Furniture Store on Main Street for our wonderful little apartment. We had everything we needed. Daddy and Annie bought a new TV from Pieratts for themselves and gave us their old Magnavox. It lasted for many years.

Our daughter, Connie Renee', was eighteen months old when I got home from Vietnam. She was afraid of me at first, but after a couple of days we were best friends; and we still are today. She was and is a wonderful singer. When she was two years old, she took a piece of paper, laid it in the floor, stood on it, and sang using a fake microphone. We have those pictures. She was so cute.

When we bought our house, Connie was five years old. We got her a dog, and she named that pup Sippy Renee White of Marshall Lane. That was her AKC registered name. She was a black and tan basset hound. She had big ears that constantly flopped when she ran and always got in her water and food. She was an outside dog and was rarely inside. Our yard was fenced to keep her in, and she did not try to get out. The problem was male dogs that got in when she was in heat. We put up an electric fence to keep them out. Now being the curious female she was, she had to smell the fence. She got her muzzle too close, and it bit her. She jumped straight up and landed between the chain link fence and the electric fence. It took a few minutes to get her into the yard again. I had to lift her over. From that point on, you could not drag her near that fence.

Carl Travis and I installed that fence, and we tested it with a cat that was walking by. Carl pushed it into the fence, and it ran the length of the yard and jumped the fence at the end without ever touching it. In general, and in principle, it worked well, except for one old male dog in the neighborhood. I built a pen to keep Sippy in when she came into heat. Well, this old dog pulled a board off the top of that pen and got in there with her. That dog got out of there before I could catch him. I went to the fire station that morning and told them about this big dog pulling the board off Sippy's pen. Moose Garrison said that dog wouldn't be hard to find because he had a hammer and crowbar in his pocket.

Later, a man, who was a Marine recruiter, had a dog named Sir Winston. When he received his orders to go overseas, he gave Winston to us. He was a huge black and white basset hound. We kept Sir Winston for quite a while. He barked all the time--day and night. He also dug up the yard and taught Sippy bad habits, so we gave him to another firefighter.

As Sippy got older, we gave her to a man who had two young girls. They had bought a farm in Jessamine County. We were worried that Sippy would be sad to leave us; but when the family came to get her, she hopped up into the back seat and sat between those two little girls and couldn't be coaxed out of that car if we had tried. She loved attention. We know she had a happy "rest of her life" there on the farm with the kids.

We also found a cat one time. It was sick, so we brought it home and nursed it back to health. One morning Lee was leaving for work and didn't know that the cat was under the tire. Well, you have heard "doggone"; well, this was "cat gone."

Fire Chief Earl R McDaniel and Jim Long were tight; and Jim, being a firefighter himself, did a lot of work for the chief. Therefore, I got to know Chief McDaniel very well. They said that if I could pass the fire department test, they would help me get on the department.

The last part of October, 1969, Chief Caton called and told me to report for training on November 3. Well, I thought Jim had somebody do this to pull a joke on me. I called Chief Caton, and he just laughed and said I was to report to work.

Before joining the fire department, I got a job at H.L. Greens to learn how to be a manager of their restaurant. Mrs. Checkers was my boss and manager of this restaurant. She was a very frugal woman and knew how to make money. I could tell you some of the tricks she used to sell her products, but you probably already know them. For example, she would take a one- or two-day-old pie, scrape off the meringue, and add new meringue to make it more presentable for that day.

One day the regional manager came to check us out. He wanted me to go to Virginia where they were opening a new restaurant, and he would train me to be manager there. Well, Mrs. Checkers said no because she needed me here. So, I missed an all-expense-paid trip to learn a trade. That put me in a bad way, and I told her she did not need me. I quit without giving her a two-week notice. I did not pass go, but I did collect my pay; and that's all she ever saw of me.

Lee had a cousin, Ed, who worked in Human Resources at IBM; and he got me a job there in 1969. I had just returned from Vietnam a year earlier, and I did not like being inside all the time. I was on the third shift boxing typewriters in Building Five. I told Ed that I was sorry, but I needed out. I don't think he ever forgave me; but he still loves it when I play Santa Claus for the family, which I have been doing since 1965.

I drove tractor trailers hauling tobacco to Wisconsin for Yeary Transfer on Christian Drive in Lexington. Then I worked for Herbert Barnes out on Newtown Pike. I loved driving that dump truck and would drive one today if I could find someone who would let me. My brother Junior who lived in Dayton, Ohio, owned a dump truck and let me drive it while we were hauling blacktop and paving a road.

Backing into a blacktop spreader takes practice and experience, and most people are not good at it. Not only do you have to back into it correctly, but as the spreader pushes you along you must keep the right amount of pressure to hold the truck wheels against the spreader. If you let the wheels get clear of the spreader, you are going to dump a load of blacktop in front of the spreader; and that's a no-no. I thought I had done a respectable job; but when the truck was empty, the man on the spreader stood up and gave me an ovation! Junior said he had never seen him do that before. I guess I am bragging, but I got a lot of experience while building and resurfacing roads around Lexington. I even helped build New Circle Road between Tates Creek Road and Richmond Road.

This is where I learned how to get a tandem truck back down when it rears up because you didn't open the tailgate soon enough while raising the bed. Yep, I was getting terribly excited when I was about ten feet in the air while Mr. Barnes' son-in-law was explaining to me how to get it down. He told me to put the truck in reverse and back it down. I did this, and the truck came right down till the front wheels were about three feet off the ground. Then it just fell to the ground, and I did not break a thing! Sounds like he had experienced this also.

Then, when I worked for Jim Long, I drove the Cat 955 with a bucket on the front. One time we put it on a trailer to move it a short distance. Jim had a bad habit of not chaining it down on the trailer and letting the motor continue to run. Well, this time the treads were muddy, and the engine was running; and I was driving the truck pulling the trailer. We backed into a driveway where standing water was in a ditch because of a water line installation. I told Jim that it was going to sink when the wheels hit it. He said just come on back, and so I did. In slow motion I watched that caterpillar slide off the trailer onto its side, and then it caught on fire. I jumped out of the truck and asked Jim if he wanted me to put it out. He quickly said, "Yes." We extinguished the fire with the extinguisher from the truck. The only thing it did was bend the fuel tank against a large fence post and break off the smokestack. Jim hooked the truck to it and pulled it back up on its tracks. We kept on working.

Like I said, I learned a lot from Jim. One winter the caterpillar's tracks were frozen and could not move. We built a fire under it, but it got too hot and set the thing on fire. Maybe he was teaching me this as part of my fire training.

Jim and June Long had two daughters who turned out to be fine women and did them proud. Vicky got married and lives in St Louis, Missouri. Sherri joined the Navy and went to Iraq. That girl can speak several languages, and I believe she worked undercover for the

Chaplaincy Service. She was in a situation and ended up badly injured. We never knew, nor did her parents, the whole story because it was all top secret. Sherri is my hero because when Obama was president and giving out awards in Atlanta, Georgia, Sherri refused to go forward to receive her award from him. No matter how hard they tried, she would not go up there. Finally, they just read the award. It said she was responsible for saving thousands of lives. What a soldier she was! Sherri doesn't remember what the incident was that injured her, but she still has nightmares.

When I worked for Jim, we did just about everything from demolition to construction of buildings, to cutting tobacco, to laying sod, and doing concrete work. You name it, and Jim did it and usually did it well.

In 1969 when I joined the Fire Department, our training consisted of modifying a house that was to be destroyed and then burn it for training. Jim couldn't wait for this to happen so he could see how I would do. I'm not sure they can do this now with all the environmental laws we have.

Back then we did not have SCBA (self-contained breathing apparatus) to protect us from the smoke, etc. We had to do the best we could. I was not a smoke eater, but that was not my problem on this fire. I sprayed the water into the building in a clockwise motion to drive the smoke away as I had been taught, but I knocked my helmet off and hot tar from the roofing fell down my neck. At this point, I ran over a couple of other recruits trying to get out of the building. With only a few blisters on my back, Jim and the trainers had a big laugh because of my panic. Most of them had been burned a time or two, so they welcomed me to the club. This was the start of a twenty-six-year career as a firefighter on the Lexington Fire Department.

I taught Driver's Training for the State Fire School when Earl R McDaniel was Lexington Fire Chief. He used many of us firefighters as trainers for these events. Charlie Feck chose me to be a driver trainer, and the course was set up in the parking lot at the UK football stadium. We made an obstacle course and let all the visiting fire companies compete in forward and reverse drills. They all enjoyed it, and I always made my training sessions fun and informative. I often see people who remember my training sessions, but I don't always remember them. I must have done something right.

From time to time we set up these trainings and competitions for our own Lexington fire companies. We kept scores to see how proficient we were from year to year. I may be bragging, but I enjoyed driving backward through the course. I think I can drive backward better than I can drive forward. I have always been a good driver since I started steering our farm vehicles at age six.

I also taught driver's training for ABC Driving School in Lexington. Sometimes that got a little scary. I taught people of every age group. I had a brake on my passenger side of the vehicle, and I had to use it a few times.

Once I was training a young boy in Winchester. At that time, the Winchester Bypass was gravel on the shoulder of the road. I asked him what would happen if he ran into the gravel, and he said that he would wreck. I grabbed the steering wheel, drove out onto the gravel, and then eased the car back up on the pavement. The boy was surprised. Next, I had him try it so he could hear the gravels hitting up under the fenders and know that he still had control of the car. This was all well and good except when he went down to take his test. He and the state police officer returned in about one minute. I asked what happened, and the trooper said he ran through a four-way stop. Well, so much for not paying attention.

When I first joined the Fire Department, everyone took their vacations in the summer months; therefore, I took mine in December between Christmas and New Year's. Lee was off from her job with the school system, and Connie was out of school during that time. We spent a few days in Gatlinburg, Tennessee. We still love going there or to Pigeon Forge several times a year.

Lt. Jim Craig was my first officer at Station 1 when I got out of basic training for firefighting. My group was the first class to attend the new training facility with its new training tower on Old Frankfort Road. The classroom building had not been built. Since I worked for Jim Long, I graded that spot with that infamous 155 Caterpillar. If you look in the creek at the end of the building, you will see a large piece of concrete that I pushed over the bank, not knowing that it was going down that far. This concrete came from the old icehouse that we tore down on Fourth Street.

We did lots of training there over the years. When some of the guys challenged this 135-pound former Marine to put up a 35-foot extension ladder with a tormentor pole, which they don't use any more, I did it. If it had been another pound heavier, I couldn't have done it!

We had a saying at the Fire Department that went like this: "We, the willing, led by the unknowing, are doing the impossible for the ungrateful. We have done so much with so little for so long, we are now qualified to do anything with nothing."

I used to jump off the tower into a net while others held it for me; and, also, I rappelled off the tower to the ground--sometimes I would shoot right through a window, which took a lot more skill, but I had learned it in the Marines.

We built smokehouses with mazes to find our way through. We used a couch, a mattress, or something that made lots of smoke when on fire and let the smoke and heat build up as we sat there and explained things to the firefighters except what happens when you stand up or spray water to upset the heat and smoke balance. It is so cool--or should I say hot--to sit there and watch the smoke build down from the ceiling. When the time was right, we had all of them stand up at the same time. When their ears hit the heat, they would drop faster than they got up. Then we showed them what happens when you introduce water into it. It upsets the balance, and you have to leave the room. This was called "Thermal Inversion." This is why people burn up in fires. When you are asleep and the smoke and heat build down from the ceiling, you get choked and sit up trying to breathe, and panic sets in. If you are asleep and smell smoke, you should roll out of bed and crawl to the door and feel to see if it is hot. If it is hot, use another exit if possible (like a window).

The Fire Department had a lot of good training to keep us safe and to help others. We had many paramedics who were the best in the country, but all the firefighters were EMTs (Emergency Medical Technicians). Currently, most Lexington firefighters are paramedics.

Though we had fun times and friendly camaraderie, there were times when we experienced sadness and heartbreak. Before we had "jaws of life" to help us get pinned people out of cars, we had to use our muscles and crowbars. One night on Russell Cave Road, two teenage boys had a car accident and were pinned against the dash and died before I could get them out. I could not sleep for several nights. Not only are you exhausted physically, but you are emotionally devastated; and it wears on you mentally.

Another sad but true incident that happened on our shift was when the EC Unit (Emergency Care) responded to a child-abuse situation. The husband and wife agreed and punished a small child by setting him on a hot electric stove because he would not stop crying. He died because of the burns he received to his buttocks, legs, and testicles. I hope those people are still in prison.

We responded to many kinds of events. This is hard to believe, but once a baby "hung" himself in the bed sheets. Twice before we had made the run and had saved him both times. The third time we were not able to save him. We couldn't believe this had happened. We were never sure that we got the full story from the parents.

We responded to lots of reports involving gunfire. We finally realized that our trucks had lower gears, and we could make a slower response till the police arrived onsite to secure the scene.

As a new recruit in the Fire Department in November, 1969, I was assigned to Station 1 on Third Street. It was one of several stations that had a pole that we used to slide down from the bedroom into the truck bay at night to make a fire run. This seems so crazy to me now, but it was a safe way to get on the truck quickly.

When you live with other firefighters for twenty-four hours at a time, you get to know them; and you get to experience a lot of different situations. I knew some of their tricks when I was new, but not all. I had heard talk about how they dumped a garbage can of water out the upper floor window at Station 1 while you sat on the apron in a chair. As you went up the stairs to see who did it, the culprit slid down the fire pole and disappeared. The apron is the area immediately in front of the doors of the firehouse. When the water hit me, I ran to the stairs but stopped to check the pole before I went up. When I got to the second floor, I heard the shower running. I checked the bedroom and anywhere else someone might hide, and then I went into the shower room. Sure enough, someone was in the shower. Usually when someone gets in the shower, he sets his night boots out. Then, if there is a fire run, he can jump into the boots, pull the britches up with the suspenders, and go. This time, the boots were a decoy because the guy in the shower just stepped in with his clothes on, turned the water on, and stood out of the way so as not to get wet. There was a hose in the deep sink that he had used to fill the trash can with water before he dumped it on me. So, I did a bad thing and used the hose to fill his boots with water; then went back down the stairs. It wasn't long before he came down and angrily said, "Look what someone did to my boots!" I said very innocently, "Look what they did to me," as I stood there soaking wet. That was the end of it.

I learned a lot from Lt. Jim Craig. It was an exciting time, and I think I learned quickly. Everything I learned was so fascinating, and I couldn't wait to learn something new. I couldn't wait to put into practice what I was learning.

I was at Station 1 about three months and then was assigned to Station 8 on North Broadway. We worked hard and played hard. Carl Travis and I were always in competition with each other--whether it was playing games or keeping Engine 8 clean and sharp. We did not have to be told what to do. Often, we did things just to see who could do it best. We kept Engine 8 shiny from bumper to bumper. Under the hood, the engine was shining. We cleaned under the fender wells as well as the frame and drive shaft under the truck. We even waxed the axle on that old machine. We were obsessed with seeing who could do it the best! We were so proud of her. She was a grand old truck, and it kept us busy and out of trouble. Well, most of the time. Currently a Lexington Firefighter, Carl Haunz, has purchased the old Maxim pumpers and displays them in Fire Prevention Parades, etc.

I have forgotten a lot about Engine 8, but Trav knew all the particulars. He had been a race car driver in his younger years, and he knew how to drive and operate that old 1,000-gallon-per-minute Maxim pumper. It was our pride and joy. I'm sure that is why after Travis died, the Training Center came up with an award in his honor, called the "One Hundred and Ten Percent Award" for new recruits. That award was so appropriately titled.

Trav and his wife, Lovelee, and their daughter, Tina, were best friends with Lee and me. We often went on vacation together. Once we borrowed Tina's car, and all of us went to Gatlinburg to ski at the newly opened ski resort. Our daughter, Connie, was young; and all five of us piled into their daughter's little Datsun with our luggage and took off. We pooled our money and knew how much we had to have to get home. So, on our way out of town headed home, we filled up with gas and bought our supper. However, on our way back to Lexington, the timing chain broke on Tina's old Datsun; and we hadn't planned for an emergency. We called Lee's brother, Junior, and he brought a trailer all the way from Annville, Kentucky, to rescue us. We were poor but happy. Mike Carr sings a song that says, "My old pappy says we're ignorant and think we're happy." It fits.

Trav and Lovelee bought a 400-acre farm in Nicholas County, and we did deer hunting there. Lee and I taught Travis how to drive a tractor on the hills and how to mow the fields with a bushhog. Some things had to be learned by doing. One time when he was mowing on top of a hill, a B-52 came over low from behind him. He nearly jumped off the tractor. Another time, a black snake wound around the brake pedal as he was mowing, and he swatted it with his glove. Those were exciting times.

We partnered with Trav and Lovelee and bought some black Angus cows. He borrowed an old truck to haul the cows from the stockyards here in Lexington to the farm. Someone told him he should not haul them in that truck, but Trav trusted the truck. When he was on the inner loop of New Circle Road and made the turn onto North Broadway, the bed of the truck fell off; and those cows scattered all over New Circle Road and North Broadway. Some of the cows went up the bank behind the service station that sat on the corner and headed down the railroad tracks. Some went up New Circle Road. The bull ended up near Russell Cave Road at the railroad tracks and was shot several times by police and put down. Others were never found. People tried to help herd them. There were sightings of cattle for a few days. Some people corralled them in their backyards and called the police to advise of their whereabouts. Travis's friend brought a trailer and picked up the ones that could be found.

Now just imagine how wild these cows were after falling off the truck. Some of them broke through fences, and sometimes we had to run from them. Once I was rounding one up that had been sighted in a pasture near Bryan Station High School, and it charged me. The grass in the field was as high as my shoulders, and I was wearing a red cap. All Lee could see was my red cap headed toward a herd of horses. I ran right into the middle of those horses, and the cow veered off in another direction. That cow was running as fast as she could, and I was running as fast as I had to. We never found that cow after that, nor did I want to.

Once the rescued cows were on the farm, Lee and I went down to round them up and give them shots. One time a cow got tangled in a barbed wire fence and tore her leg badly. We cleaned it, bandaged it, and gave her penicillin. Another time when we got there, Trav was trying to round them up for us by waving a burlap bag at them. The cows didn't know what to do. Then we got a bucket of feed and walked them into the barn. These were Angus cows and are wild by nature. You can imagine how they reacted to a sack waving in the air. But we all had a great time on the farm, and we still laugh about our experiences.

When I first arrived at Station 8, I was told that I had to be on the truck in three seconds after the alarm sounded. So, I was wired up. After I went to bed, they crept in and put the suspenders of my night boots in between the boots instead of on the outside of each boot as I had them. Now you may not know this, but there is no way you can get those suspenders over your shoulders when they are in that position. When the alarm sounded, I panicked and feared the truck might leave without me. I jumped around and crawled to get on the tailboard of Engine 8. It just so happened that this was right after Valentine's Day, and Lee had given me new white boxer shorts with big red hearts on them. So here I was with my britches down and my new shorts showing as I stood on the tailboard of Engine 8. I wondered why we weren't going anywhere. Then they all started laughing, and I knew I'd been had. Those guys never let me forget that.

In the middle of all the hilarious situations, there were serious events that required our total attention and professionalism. On North Broadway near Loudon Avenue there are two-story apartments that line the street. As we arrived on the scene, flames were coming out of some of the windows. We observed a woman in the window of one of the upstairs apartments with a baby in her arms. The flames in the room behind her were visible. We firefighters are professionals, but it takes time to get a ladder from the truck to the window. The woman was just about ready to jump. A firefighter ran over beneath the window and advised her to toss the baby down to him. She did and he caught it. By that time, we were putting the ladder in place. She yelled, "Can I come down now?" As I climbed the ladder to help her, she climbed out onto the ladder; and we descended to safety. As she took her baby in her arms, she thanked us as we were putting the fire out in the apartment building. We saved the building as well.

At an apartment fire in Winburn subdivision, a woman's dog was still inside as she escaped the fire. She was hysterical over the dog. A young man went into the fire and brought her dog out. The woman grabbed the dog from him and didn't even thank the young man who had to be taken by the EC Unit to the hospital for burns on his hands and smoke inhalation. I felt badly for this young man and was angry with the woman because she was so ungrateful to him.

One July 4, there was a fireworks show at North Park Shopping Center. All of us, except Capt. Charlie Feck, climbed on top of the station to watch. The phone rang, and Capt. Feck answered it. It was Patsy, Lt. Wilson's wife. Capt. Feck walked all the way around the firehouse looking for Lt. Wilson. He finally told her he couldn't find Wilson. When Feck was walking and hollering for Wilson, we all lay down on the roof so he couldn't see us. Later when we came down, we got a good chewing out! We did a lot of other bad things but never that again.

Lt. Richard Wilson was at Station 8 when I came there. He was from Powell County, Kentucky, which is in Eastern Kentucky. His dad was a gynecologist. They lived in a house with very little grass in the yard. The soil is hard, and it's difficult to grow grass or anything else on those hills.

One day at the firehouse one of the guys discovered that he could throw an egg in the air in a certain way, and it would not break when it landed. We all were amazed and started doing it. Before long we were throwing eggs in the air, and 90 percent of the time they would not break. Now let me explain how this works. You can do it to impress your friends most of the time. Find a lawn that has a good stand of grass without rocks or objects for the egg to land on. Put your index finger on the end of an egg. As you throw it, spin it backwards as fast as you can. When it hits the grass, it will bounce but not break unless it hits a pebble or something hard. We threw eggs all the way across the firehouse into the front yard, and they just bounced. Now if you try to eat this egg later, it is already scrambled.

The rest of the story is this: When Lt. Wilson went home to see his mom in Powell County, he wanted to impress her with this egg-throwing trick. He took a dozen eggs out of the fridge and went out to the yard. Now, remember, they had very little grass. His mom stopped him about the eleventh egg before he broke the entire dozen. We had a big laugh when he came back to the station and told us the story. We never understood what he didn't understand about the grass.

We had lots of fun with Lt. Richard Wilson, and he was a good fire officer and became a fire captain. He told us a story about travelling in Eastern Kentucky. He passed a park where a family reunion was taking place. He turned the car around and went back, walked up, and joined in the conversation with some of the people. Before long he was part of the family. He had a wonderful meal with his new family. Who knows, up there they might have been family.

One time Capt. Luther Stivers, Travis, and I were on business inspections. We took a break at the Congress Inn across from Station 8. Travis was the driver at the time; and he stayed with the truck, which was parked on a slope in the parking lot. Capt. Stivers and I checked out the railroad tracks behind the Congress Inn. Travis was standing outside the truck on the right-hand side, and I slipped into the driver's seat and released the emergency brake. When Travis saw the truck rolling, he was scrambling to get into the driver's seat. We laughed and laughed. What good times we had. Except the time when we pulled out of the station and saw flames coming through the roof of the Congress Inn. I almost fell through that roof trying to put the fire out. My angels were still on the job.

The Fire Prevention Parade was always a big deal, and we went all out to make Station 8 look good. We put things together that looked like an old steam pumper. It looked so good that many people thought it was real. We even dressed in old uniforms that would have been worn in the 1800s. We used smoke grenades in the smokestack. We almost choked the Girl Scouts who marched in the parade behind us. This thing looked so good that Barbourville, Kentucky, asked us to bring it down to their parade. We loved it.

One day Al Harris, Travis, one other firefighter, and I went to Lawrenceburg to play golf. We are all so competitive all the time. Al and Travis made a bet that the one who lost had to walk back to Lexington. Well, Travis lost; and we drove off and left him standing there. When we got back to Lexington, would you believe there he was walking up the street within 100 yards of his house. He beat us back to Lexington after catching a ride. The joke was on us.

We had so much fun on and off duty. We were like a huge family.

Lee was always involved in the FD Ladies Auxiliary, and at one time was their president. They got together meals for the firefighters when they were out fighting fires for extended periods. They had lots of fundraisers. And they always had a float in the Fire Prevention Parade, also. What wonderful memories for the kids in their costumes riding on the floats.

The Ladies Auxiliary had small pins to wear that said LFD Ladies Auxiliary, and they looked very much like a miniature police badge. One day Lee was working at the Fayette County Schools and was called out to assist a bus driver who was having discipline problems on her bus. When Lee entered the bus and called to get their attention, one little fellow near the front reported to the others that "she's a lady cop." The little perps went peacefully onto the "Bread Box" with Lee and back to the garage to await their parents' arrival to take them home. Lee never told them differently. It worked that time, so she wore the badge a lot after that.

One day in 1974, tornadoes came through Kentucky causing a lot of damage. I was on duty at Station 8 on North Broadway the night the tornado came through wiping out several neighborhoods in several states including Lexington and neighboring towns. Stamping Ground was hit hard. Lee and Connie spent the night in the bathroom. (You may ask why the bathroom? It is because it is the strongest room in the house. The tub is strong, and the walls are 2 X 6 rather than 2 X 4 so that pipes and wires can be run through them.) Lee made Connie a bed of blankets in the bathtub, and Lee lay on the floor, beside the tub. Connie thought it was a neat idea. Lee listened to the police and fire scanner all night. Sometime after that experience, we dug an emergency shelter under the house since we do not have a basement. We poured a concrete floor, and the walls and top are pine. We also have emergency supplies down there.

The next day after the tornado, some of us Lexington firefighters went to some smaller towns to help with their emergencies since their responders had worked many hours without relief. Helping others is what firefighting is all about. They were trying to get an old military generator started; and being a jokester, I told them to push it. If you are blonde, you might not get that.

Many barns were destroyed, so there was a need to get these rebuilt. The Chrisman brothers, Lee's cousins from Sand Gap, Kentucky, whom I mentioned earlier, were builders and started building these barns. I started helping them, and that was another experience in my long list of jobs.

When putting rails or stringers in the barns, we learned to throw a hatchet about twelve to fourteen feet and catch it by the handle. This hatchet was used to cut notches in the rails. We used forklifts to raise the metal roofing up to where we could put it on the roof. Sometimes the hydraulic fluid would leak out on the metal roofing. Now you can imagine how slick that would be on the metal. Well, one day I stepped out on the metal but did not see the hydraulic fluid on it. My foot slipped, and I began to slide toward the edge of the roof. I reached over with my claw hammer to stop myself from falling about twenty-five feet to the ground. Remember those three angels? Well, they were there also. This was at Richmond Road and Old Kentucky Route 25.

One night a man's car quit in front of Station 8, and the man came walking into the kitchen and saw Travis. He asked him if he could give him a jump. Trav said, "Yes," and jumped up in the air. I was standing at the kitchen sink; and Trav said, "How about you, Goob?" (They called me Goob because of Gomer Pyle in the USMC TV Series.) So, I jumped up in the air also. That guy never cracked a smile, so we went out and started his car and he left. He must have thought we were crazy. Some people just have no sense of humor.

One time in my early years at Station 8, I went to bed early one night. My bed was next to the living room wall where the TV was, and one of the firefighters waited until I got to sleep and then did something that upset me greatly. It hadn't been that long since I had returned from Vietnam. He backed up next to that wall just inches away from my head and beat on the wall with both his fists really hard. This scared me and made my heart beat fast. I went to the captain and asked him to advise them not to do that again, but just in a few minutes they did it again. Now, I'm not a bad guy; and you don't want to really get me going, so I put a stop to it. I got out of bed, dressed, and prepared to stay up all night. I waited until this guy got to sleep, and I grabbed his bed and shook the fire out of it! He got mad and said I was acting like a child. I said, "Okay, but you are going to sit up all night with this child." I was ready to fight. Suffice it to say, neither of us got any sleep that night. But the incident never happened again.

When I came onto the Fire Department in 1969, there was a man in Lexington named Garvis Kincaid who cared for the families on the department. He was a very generous man. Every year at Christmas he gave every firefighter a case of grapefruit which he bought from the local schools that sold them as fundraisers. It benefitted the firefighters as well as the schools.

Mr. Kincaid was a banker who lived on East Main Street. When I worked with Gene Williamson in his appliance repair business, we went to Mr. Kincaid's beautiful home to repair the refrigerator. They had lovely antiques. I was always thankful for him and Kerr Brothers Funeral Home because they gave us gifts each Christmas. One year they gave us keychain nail clippers in a little plastic case that you could carry in your pocket. When Mr. Kincaid died, the gifts soon stopped coming. When the plastic on my clippers wore out, I looked everywhere for a replacement because I was so used to having it. There was not one to be found. When I started working with leather, I made my own case. Now I always have my clippers in my pocket, and I have also given them as gifts.

Station 8 housed Engine 8, Ladder 3, and Emergency Care 3. One day, the fire bell rang, and Travis was in the back room washing out a mop in the deep sink and did not hear the bell. I still laugh thinking about this story. The EC unit was out on a call, so we only had the ladder and engine companies going. We jumped on the truck. Now Travis was assigned to drive this day. We changed drivers every two weeks. Capt. Stivers was in the front seat, and Larry Courtney and I were in the back. The engine always leads the ladder truck, but no one could go because Travis would not get on the truck. We were all hollering for him to come on, but I can still see him standing in the door of the station with a mop in his hand with a look on his face that says, "You ain't tricking me!" Courtney and I started laughing, and this made things worse. Finally, Capt. Stivers told me to get up front and drive. When we started to turn on Broadway, Trav threw that mop down, ran, and jumped on the back of Ladder 3. When we were ready to return to the station, Capt. Stivers said with that southern drawl he has, "Trav, do you want to ride back with us?" We called Capt. Stivers "Cool Hand Luke."

One night about 1 a.m. we were called to Loudon Square Restaurant on the corner of North Broadway and Loudon Avenue. As we parked in the middle of Broadway, Travis and I, who were rookies at the time, were like two Chihuahua puppies. We were ready to pull the hose off the back of the truck and go to work. Capt. Stivers said in his slow drawl, "Just wait a minute, boys, and let me see what's going on." Capt. Stivers walked between the buildings to see where we were needed. Then he came back and told us what to do and where to go. Oh, did I tell you that flames were coming from the back of the building, and he wanted to confirm where we needed to lay our hose line. We laid hose and successfully put out the fire. You just don't get any better training than this.

While at Station 6 at Scott and Upper streets, we had a restaurant fire on Euclid Avenue. It was well involved when we arrived. Back then we had just started getting SCBA (Self-Contained Breathing Apparatus) on the trucks, but I did not put one on. I walked all the way through the building with fire all around me. There was just something about the flames that made me keep going till I came out the front of the restaurant. It did get a little scary toward the end because the fire was gaining ground all the time. We did put it out, but I think it was a total loss.

Sometimes we did things without thinking how it looked to the public. One case in point was our EC Unit responding to a 10/46, injury accident. Our engine company was closest to the incident, so we responded and arrived on the scene first but determined an ambulance was not needed. We were returned to regular duty on 10/7 status and returned to quarters. In this case, it was about lunch time, so we turned off our lights and siren and pulled into McDonald's to pick up lunch. I admit this didn't look good. A lady called in and reported that the engine had made an emergency run to get lunch. As a result, we were retrained to go around the block before we stopped for lunch in a situation like that.

In defense of our EC Units, they are out on calls so much that sometimes they might need to do that in order to get a meal.

Speaking of meals, it never failed that when we prepared a big meal for everyone at the firehouse and it was just about time to eat, the fire bell would ring and here we go again. We did learn to never throw leftovers away until the next morning because they were very tasty after a 2 a.m. working fire. I remember at Station 8 that usually one man made breakfast for all of us. We took turns. This was a lot of fun and introduced all of us to different meals and the way to prepare them. All of this stopped, however, when one firefighter dropped a glob of butter on the toe of his shoe and then scraped it up and threw it back in the skillet.

Cold weather could be a real problem for fire engines. As you know, water freezes at 32 degrees F. Well, there are a lot of nights and days in the winter where the temperature is well below that here in Lexington, Kentucky. Pumps must be drained, and the connection threads have to be treated with water displacement. Trucks freeze to the ground from all the water being used around them. Hoses were not shut off completely to keep the water from freezing in the hoses.

This just gives you an idea of some of the things we had to deal with at the fire station and on the fire scene.

In the early 1970s Capt. Charlie Feck came up with the idea of fire gate numbers. Every entrance from the city outward on every road was assigned a number beginning with "One" to ever how many numbers were needed for that road to the end of the county line. Even gates into fields were given numbers to help in the event accidents might occur at that location. I was one of the first firefighters to be assigned to place these number signs on a post or fence. Several times we responded to gates where there were accidents with farm equipment. These fire gate locators were very beneficial. Other counties adopted this system as well.

Charlie Feck and Carol lived on Twelfth Street. One day he placed on the curb a large can filled with debris which they had picked up from around their property. It contained bricks and pieces of broken concrete. They were sitting on the porch when a man and woman came by on a motorcycle. Now this dude must have been showing off because he kicked the can and almost wrecked. Before the cyclist got down to North Broadway, Charlie jumped up and yelled, "Come back and kick it again!"

Kentucky is a tobacco state and in the spring of the year farmers used to burn wood on their tobacco beds to kill the weeds and pests before sowing the seeds. Sometimes someone would complain about the smell of smoke, and we would go out and put their fire out. It's just not built into me to destroy someone's livelihood, so I would stand and visit with the farmer until it burned down. We never did get another call that someone was choking to death, so I guess we did okay.

Years ago, before North Park was developed, it was farmland on the side of Russell Cave Road between New Circle Road and North Broadway. One day Engine 8 got a call that there was a grass fire, but there was no address. There was a McDonald's nearby, and we stopped there to try to locate a way to get to the fire. Finally, we found a small entrance in a fencerow and started up the dirt path to get to the smoke. Well, when we stopped at McDonald's, firefighter Kip Kalby did not get back inside the fire truck. He rode on the tailboard (we rode this way sometimes back then). There were a few rough spots on this dirt road, and Kalby lost his grip and footing and fell off. Capt. Stivers looked back and said, "I think we lost Kip." When I looked through the mirror, I saw Kip rolling in the dust. We stopped and helped him back on the truck and proceeded to put out the fire. At least Luther and I did. It was a couple of weeks before Kip could do much firefighting, but we covered for him.

One day I turned left onto Winburn Drive from Russell Cave Road and Capt. Stivers' door flew open. I grabbed him to keep him from falling out. The trucks did not have seat belts at that time. It seemed like every day was a challenge and sometimes fun.

We had a water fight one day, and it ended up in the bathroom which had a door from both sides. Mike Sunley and I had Moose Garrison trapped, and Mike had a big cup of water to throw on Moose. This was not Moose's first big fight because he used to be a bouncer at Marty's Bar on Richmond Road. So, without hesitation, Moose smacked that cup of water up into Mike's face. Mike must have been taking a breath at the time because he began choking while Moose left the scene. I could not chase Moose because I needed to stay and help Mike who was still choking.

One morning about 2 a.m. we made a fire run to a house just off Georgetown Street. There were flames shooting out the roof (what we called "bloomed out"); and as we were laying hose and hooking the truck to the fire hydrant, one of the firefighters needed a bathroom badly. He went into the house, kept his mask on, laid his SCBA tank down by the commode, and took care of business. Sometimes "you just gotta do what you gotta do." Then he helped us put the fire out. Firefighters had to be able to think on the go.

We pulled pranks on each other all the time. One prank was dumping cold water on someone when he was in the shower. Another prank was catching someone on the toilet, raising the window, and wetting him down with the garden hose. Once, a person was in the shower feeling good till someone dumped cold water on top of him. Now the real fun starts because he wanted to find out who did this so he could get payback. He jumped out of the shower and chased a guy through the living room where there just happened to be another firefighter sitting on the couch with his wife. Too late; she had been mooned. No turning back now; he just keeps on going. With those wet feet on the tile floor, I am certainly glad he didn't try to stop. I'm sure he would have slipped and fallen.

One time Bing Robinson fell part way through a burned-out floor. He was lying on his back with his SCBA on and couldn't get up. I just happened to find him while searching through the smoke and fire and pulled him out before the flames got to him. He was very thankful.

One afternoon we responded to a call in Griffin Gate, a very exclusive gated community. As a matter of fact, my good friend and blood brother, Nelson Hix, built several of those homes. Some of them are very elegant and some even have storm/bomb shelters. Back to the EC run, the call was concerning an elderly female who was having a heart attack. The Station 10 EC Unit was on another call, so another EC unit from farther away was dispatched. My Engine 10 Company was on its own. As we approached the entrance gate, there was no guard on duty; and the gate was closed. A long wooden arm served as a barrier, and we could not get around it. We needed to proceed several hundred yards beyond the gate to reach the residence. We knew that mere seconds could make a difference in life or death. To get through the gate, I jumped out of the truck and broke off the wooden arm. When it snapped, I fell backward on my buttocks and almost turned a backward flip. I learned to tumble in high school. I got back on the truck, and we proceeded on the call. The lady was, in fact, having a heart attack. We did CPR until the EC Unit arrived, and she survived. Nothing was ever said about the broken gate.

I like to tell the story about an oil tank fire at a refinery in Texas. A large fuel tank was ablaze for a long time. All fire departments have what is called a "mutual aid" policy. This is where other departments can be called in to help when things get too big to handle. In this case, several fire departments had been called, but the fire was still out of control. They called in a little volunteer fire department from out in the country. Its old fire truck with about fifteen firefighters hanging all over it drove past all the other units right up to the fire, pulled the hose, and put out that fire. The owners of the oil company were so grateful that they called all the firefighters with this truck and gave their department a gift of $25,000. Well, the media was there taking notes of everything and asked the captain how they were going to use this money. "Well," the captain said, "I don't know what we will do with all of it, but the first thing we are going to do is get the brakes fixed on the truck!"

Another story about Texas is that a firefighter went on vacation to Houston. He went to a restaurant and bar and ordered a small steak and a small beer. When the waiter came with the steak, it was hanging out over the platter; and the firefighter said, "That's not my steak because I ordered a small steak." The server said, "Yes, Sir, that is yours because everything is big here in Texas." He said, "Well, okay then." But when they brought the beer, it was in a large pitcher with foam running all out the top. He said, "This can't be mine because I ordered a small beer." Again, the server said, "Yes, Sir, it for sure is yours because everything is big here in Texas." He started eating that steak and drinking that beer and soon had to go to the men's room. He asked the waiter where it was and was told to go down the hallway to the third door on the left. But he went down to the third door on the right and fell into the swimming pool. Every time he came up, he was yelling, "Don't flush it! Don't flush it!" Alaskans got so tired of hearing how big Texas is that they threatened that if Texas didn't quit bragging, they would split Alaska in half; and then Texas could brag about being the third largest state!!

We do tell lots of funny stories at the firehouse, and we do tell lots of real-life occurrences as well. When we got back to the firehouse after being off for forty-eight hours, we couldn't wait to hear what had happened those days on and off duty.

Joe Best and John Gosper were my two firefighters on Engine 10. Then Kristin Chilton came to our truck out of basic training. I told Kristin that I was not excited about women firefighters, but it was a reality; and I could deal with it, or like my wife says, "just get over it". We got along great, however, and none of us had any problems; and we always worked well together. They all knew their jobs and I never had to remind them.

Everybody on Engine 10 was more educated and smarter than I. Joe Best was a Lieutenant in the Army Reserves as a tank commander. I once told Joe I would never stand in his way. John Gosper was from the Northeast and was also highly educated. Kristin had more degrees than a thermometer. All of them were very intelligent and had common sense, too, which is why they were good in Hazardous Materials.

After I retired, Kristin Chilton became the Chief of the Lexington Fire Department; and Joe and John were chiefs under her command. I was proud to be in the same ranks with them. I believe the Fire Department has done very well under their leadership. I guess I just had to retire and let them advance in their careers, and advance they did.

I volunteered to cut the firefighters' hair at the station. Kristin's hair was long, black, very coarse, and hard to keep up under the fire helmet. Sometimes the powers that be would complain about her hair, and I had to defend her. That happened once after we had been lying under a mobile home kicking out the insulation to get water on a fire. We all thought we were about to drown as there was very little space under the mobile home. If I had any hair, mine would have been down, too.

I always said Kristin was my best driver because she never scared me like Joe and John did. John got there fast but scared me half to death, and Joe acted like he couldn't see past the hood of the truck. We made a tight team. I was always so proud of these guys. They made me look good. I tried to always be a mentor, but sometimes they mentored me.

Occasionally, we responded to calls with an active shooting in progress. It didn't take many of these calls for us to learn to back off and let the Police Department get around us. We didn't carry guns, and all we had for defense was water and a pike pole.

Once I thought I was going to be involved in a shooting when we were on house inspections. Mike Sunley snuck out ahead of me and went into a friend's house. When I knocked on the door and announced, "Fire Department," he hollered back some bad words and said, "Get away from here before I blow your head off!" As I watched that door open, I ran so fast a bullet couldn't have caught me. There was a big laugh at my expense, but that was just another day on duty at Fire Station 8.

One time the police were chasing a young man on Charlotte Court, and he ran into a building; however, a different fellow ran out. He was also a young man. He got shot in the leg and our truck and EC Unit were called to the scene. Later, there were riots over this incident. When we arrived, a crowd began to form around the man. Things were starting to turn ugly fast, so without doing much triage, I told my men to put him on the stretcher and head to the EC Unit about 50 yards away as fast as possible. We got him safely into the ambulance, and they left the scene for the hospital. The police had several units on the scene. As my men and I climbed into the truck and started to leave, I looked out the window to see that we and the police were surrounded by a mob of angry people. They were closing in, throwing trash cans, rocks, or anything else they could get their hands on. We were totally blocked and couldn't move. The news media had arrived, and they were in our line of escape as well. I looked out the window and saw a man hit a female police sergeant on the side of her head with a brickbat. I jumped out of the truck and helped her to my seat in the truck while the police tried to hold off the mob. She was bleeding and was barely conscious. I held her in my seat and told the driver to go. I blew the siren and air horn as loudly as they would go, and the crowd just fell back. We were able to get her out of there. My plan was to clear the area and have another EC Unit respond to transport her to the hospital. Since this would take more time, which I didn't think we had, I told my driver to head to St. Joseph Hospital and advised our dispatch about our intentions.

When we got back on duty and back to the station house, Chief McComas called me and said that if I was going to use that truck as an ambulance, we needed to take the hose off! I am glad that he knew that I made the right decision because time was so important for her. Chief McComas was a great Fire Chief, and the Fire Department did well under his leadership.

A few days later a detective came to the station and gave us credit for getting things under control because when we blew those horns and siren so loudly, those rioters fell back; and the police were able to form a defensive line and get things under control. Later, that police sergeant had a lot of medical problems and finally had to take disability. This really hurt when I heard about it. I wished I could have done more.

One day we got a call to respond to a concrete plant with a tower on Newtown Pike. A young man had climbed the tower and was threatening to jump. I was on Aerial 3 at the time, and they thought they might be able to use Aerial 3's ladder to get him down. We parked out of the way and stayed back in the shadows and watched as the police worked to coax him down. I noticed he was wearing a USMC sweatshirt. Since I was a former Marine, I asked permission to start a conversation with the young man. They said, "Sure." I walked up and yelled to him, "Semper Fi" (Always Faithful). That young fellow started cursing and said those "blankety blanks" wouldn't let him in the Marines!! So, I backed out quickly and let the police deal with him.

They did get him down without injury to himself or anyone. I'm sure they took him to get some mental help.

When we worked as firefighters or police officers, there was always danger around us. We must have been crazy to do these jobs because when everyone else is running out of buildings that are on fire, we are trying to get in. Remember the New York Twin Towers and the World Trade Center before that.

One day we were on I-75 North at an auto fire on the right side of the road. I looked up to see a tractor trailer hauling prefab trusses coming toward us. The trusses were sticking way out on the right side of the trailer and were going to hit our truck and us if he did not change lanes. I jumped into the lane waving furiously and jumping up and down to get his attention. Just in the nick of time, he moved over enough to miss us. Thank you, my three angels.

One time we were on the outer loop of New Circle Road between Newtown and Georgetown Road. An older lady was going in the same direction we were going but she was on the inner loop going toward Georgetown Road. I told the driver to go across the grass in the median and get in front of her with our lights and sirens on full blast to keep her from getting hit head on. We got her headed in the right direction and thought no more about it until we got a nice recognition letter from City Hall. It so happened that another lady saw the incident and contacted the city to inform them of our good deed because her mother had been killed in a head-on collision. There are still good people in the world.

One of the most beneficial things we did on duty was business inspections, which we took very seriously. Once we had been in a building doing an inspection, we knew what the business handled, how to do a pre-attack, and what we were likely to deal with when we arrived on scene. It helps to know what the floor plan looks like before you get an emergency call to that location. We had a good idea of what might happen and were aware of the dangers. All this information came to mind if we needed to respond to that address. We all discussed this information on the way to the scene and were able to relay known information to the other units making that call as well.

We had Emergency Guidebooks to help us with transportation incidents. That's why there are Haz-Mat placards on transport vehicles.

We also had professors and chemists on call to help us determine what might happen in a given situation. I always told my men that if we pulled up to an accident involving a tractor trailer rig and the driver was running across a field away from the incident that we should fall right in behind him. Obviously, he knew something we didn't.

Often the police arrived on the scene first, and we called them our "coptometer."

We learned how to contain liquids by building "over-dams" and "under-dams" and how to stay uphill and upwind from the emergency.

A man and woman lived behind the firehouse, and they were childhood friends with Chief McDaniel. The lady was so particular that our men could not park their personal trucks behind the station next to her property, which was separated by a large hedgerow. As a result, the firefighters had to park their trucks across the street at a motel. However, if they drove their cars, they could park behind the firehouse.

This lady watched our station constantly, and we could do nothing without her knowing it. One day we decided to have a little fun while we were having a CPR class in the room facing this lady's house. We made sure the blinds were open during this class. In this class we use a dummy that we call "Sussi-Annie" to practice CPR and breathing. Now, "Sussi-Annie" has no clothing, and the rubber looks like pink skin. We held her up and danced around the room. A few minutes later we got a call from downtown wanting to know what we were doing. We told them we were having a CPR class.

This same lady would not allow any basketball playing behind the station, even though we had a goal back there. Eventually, we had to take the hoop down so it wouldn't be used. I should be so ashamed of myself, but one morning at 6:30 a.m. I thought I would do a little experiment. Another firefighter and I grabbed the goal that was stored in the back room, ran out with a ladder, and put one bolt in to hold it. As I did that, she was on the other side of the hedge hollering, "Mr. Fireman, Mr. Fireman." We did not feel obliged to respond because a fireman stokes the boilers on the train and firefighters put out fires. We paid no attention, jumped down, and ran into the firehouse. She headed to her house. We then ran back out and took the hoop down. By the time we got back inside, the phone was ringing from Central

Station. The Chief wanted to know why we had a basketball goal out back. After getting a good chewing out by the Chief, the Captain got off the phone and went to look for himself. He saw there was no hoop on the post. He was just about to call the Chief and tell him how crazy our neighbor was, but we confessed. Captain Stivers was not too upset because he knew the situation we had to deal with.

Another time Captain Wilson was down on his knees reaching through the hedge to retrieve a golf ball, and there she was looking at him--eyeball to eyeball! She marched straight into her house and called our firehouse phone number and demanded to talk with the man in charge. We put the captain, who had been looking at her, on the phone. She complained to him, and he apologized for our actions and assured her he would take care of the offender!

I spent a few years at Station 6 at Scott and Upper streets. This was close to the University of Kentucky, so we had a lot of the UK students in and out or just walking by on their way to class.

We saw a lot of interesting things going on in the area just in front of the UK Administration Building and Buell Armory. As a matter of fact, I used to take karate classes at the Buell Armory under Sin Tae back in the early 70s. I almost tripped over some lovers one dark night as I walked through the grass from class on my way back to Station 6 where I had parked.

A man who lived on Prall Street and worked at Good Samaritan Hospital often came by the firehouse to bring us pies that were the best I have ever eaten. He was a great cook. He also made peach brandy wine. Some people said it was very good. I still have one of his bottles of wine. That was probably in the 70s. I won't tell you some of the pranks we played on him, but he loved firefighters and policemen. If you had to go to the hospital, he would see to it that you had everything you needed. We called him "Sweet Evening Breeze."

We played a lot of ping pong at Station 6. Ray Glass was probably one of the best ping pong players on the entire department. As Captain Wheeler and another firefighter were playing ping pong, the other guy's paddle slipped out of his hand and broke an eight-foot fluorescent bulb which was just above the table. Before the glass stopped falling, Captain Wheeler threw his paddle up and broke the other bulb. After the shock of it all, we had a big laugh. Captain Wheeler was always laid back, and this was not something we would think he would do. Then we replaced the bulbs and cleaned up the mess. Those bulbs needed to be changed anyway.

We always had fun even over little things like firefighter John Logdon jumping up on the couch every time he saw a snake on TV. When he was a child, a copperhead struck at him and hung its fangs in the buckle on his boot. Every step he took as he was running, the snake hit his other leg. I think I'd be getting on high ground, too, if it were me.

We had an EC Unit that ran out of Station 6, and the two firefighters on it were a great team and worked well together. I know they saved a lot of lives. And they always came back to the station with a funny story or lots of times it was a life-threatening situation. One time they pulled up to a shooting at a bar at Sixth Street and Limestone before the police arrived. Someone chased them around the EC Unit with a knife. Thankfully, the police arrived soon and took charge.

One of these EMTs was prone to "odoriferate," and the other guy had to smell all this. While they were at the traffic light at Limestone and Euclid, he jumped out of the EC Unit and started fanning the door in a way that everyone would know what he was doing. They were not on an emergency run at the time.

One time I was assigned to an EC Unit, and we were on a run about 2 a.m. As we headed back to the station, we passed Station 5 on the way. Earlier that night a girl from a bar down the street had jumped into a friend's car and drove off. When she turned into the apron at Station 5 to turn around, she could not reach the brake and crashed into the big glass overhead door. This knocked out some of the glass and bent it so badly that it had to be replaced. Our maintenance guys fixed it temporarily to get through the night. We had all heard about this happening, so when we stopped at the red light at Maxwell and Woodland, I jumped out of the truck and ran over to the damaged door while the men were upstairs sleeping. I wanted them to think this was happening again so I ran up to the door, which must have been in a bind and under stress, and I beat on it to make a lot of noise. Boy, did it ever make a noise! Glass started falling everywhere. I ran back to the

EC Unit, and we got out of there. Nothing was ever said about it, so now I'm coming clean.

We had an EC Unit make a run to a man who was knocked out with a big gash in his forehead. The story is this: When the lady of the house went to the store, her husband was under the car working on the exhaust. When she returned, he was still there. She had eaten part of a red snow cone, so she lifted his belt and stuck it down in his trousers and ran into the house laughing. But she met her husband coming down the hall. They ran back outside to find the neighbor who had come to assist. He had knocked himself out when he set up and hit the underside of the car. As the EC Unit was loading this guy onto the stretcher, they discovered all this red wet stuff on the front of his jeans. While she was explaining it all, they got to laughing so hard they dropped him off the stretcher and banged him all up. When he got to the hospital he woke up with a gash on his head, red wet trousers, and bleeding from the scrapes on his leg. He had no clue what had happened. Just another day at the Fire Department.

At a bar we picked up a man who needed to go to the hospital on the EC Unit. I'm not sure what his problem was, but there was a woman with him whom he had just met. She didn't even know his name but rode to the hospital with him. When we got there, she gave this stranger her last $2. She insisted he have it. As soon as I could, I slipped her a $5 bill. I had tears in my eyes over that incident.

Firefighters were constantly training, sometimes in class at the station or out for driver training. Other times we would be practicing rappelling at the training center tower. One of our funeral home directors was teaching a class at Station 6 to certify us as CPR trainer Instructors. Now I was kind of hard-headed but was always willing to learn, but I wanted to have a good time while doing it.

One instructor had scenarios written on pieces of folded paper. We could not open ours until he called us to come up front and read it aloud to the class. Then we explained what actions we would take. Now, the night before, I had been reading some jokes in *Reader's Digest*. Being the jokester that I am, I decided to share one with the class. When the instructor called on me, I opened my paper and just acted like I was reading his scenario. It went like this: "As the hunter sat by the tree, he looked up and saw the buck. He took two quick shots; but before he could get the cork back in the bottle, the deer had fled." That's when I found out the instructor could not take a joke because he expelled me from the class! I don't know why I am always getting expelled from something. Captain Wheeler was so mad about this; but not at me, for he thought it was funny, too. We were short on trainers, and Captain Wheeler needed me so badly. But that was not to be. Afterwards, I was glad that I did not finish the class because they worked those guys so hard, on duty and off duty.

Sometimes firefighters could get distracted, and we loved playing jokes on each other. It seemed that just about all of us had been wet down by the sprayer on the kitchen sink. All it took was a rubber band around the lever on the sprayer and then aim it toward where someone might stand when they turned the water on. They were soaked down before they could turn the water off. One firefighter said that there was no way we could get him wet that night. Well, we staged something that really got his mind distracted. Within five minutes he was soaked. He was a good sport and said that we got him good that time. The bet was that he had to kiss someone's back side, and he paid off.

This is the same firefighter who was in a small dark office talking to his wife on the phone one day. I jerked the door open and started shooting my blank .22 pistol. I yelled, "Mess with my wife, will you?" He threw the telephone, jumped up, and almost tore up the office. We played some bad jokes on each other.

We laid a lot of fire hose for training when we were at the fire training center on Old Frankfort Pike. I was on Engine 6 with Captain Wheeler and Ray Glass. We had laid a forward lay and had about 300 feet of hose laid out. We were in the process of loading it back onto the truck. Captain Wheeler wanted to drag the hose to the truck and load it, but I wanted to back the truck to the hose and load it that way. We did it my way, and Captain Wheeler never said anything. He could have disciplined me or given me a write-up, but he didn't. I really did feel bad after that. I learned a great lesson, and I remembered that incident many years later when I became an officer and had to work with my firefighters.

As a captain, I wrote up a firefighter on his fitness report. I wanted him to know what I did and why, so I went to him and explained the situation. When I finished, he said I could kiss his rear end. Immediately, I thought back to the Captain Wheeler situation; and so, I did nothing more about it. However, he did show improvement after that.

Another time at Station 8 we made a fire run to Hollow Creek. When we arrived, we had smoke showing from a couch on fire outside the house. As Captain Stivers climbed out of the truck, a man came toward him cursing because he had just spent $100 on smoke detectors; and now, they were destroyed. He was blaming the captain for his loss. But Captain Stivers stepped up in his face and said, "Don't start no 'stuff' with me." He used another word, however, and the guy backed down. We laid hose and put out his fire. But he did have a lot of damage.

In early 1990, the Lexington Fire Department started dealing with HazMat (Hazardous Materials Emergencies) for Fayette County. We had three or four stations that participated in this program. We did a lot of Haz-Mat training in Kentucky as well as other states like Florida and Washington, D.C. Professionals also came here to train us (i.e. Safety Systems from Jacksonville, Florida). We trained every Thursday night whether we were on duty or not. We learned a lot of chemistry and what might happen if some products got together. We learned what to do in that case and how to protect ourselves and others when unexpected situations occurred. We learned how to don our safety suits quickly and how much protection we would need depending on the situation we were dealing with. We knew how to decontaminate ourselves and our team members in the event of a spill of a hazardous substance. We had decontamination pools we used for this. These decontamination pools had to be set up before we entered the danger zone to deal with a situation. There were four levels of protective clothing--A, B, C, and D. "A" level was the most protection and required that we wear the fully encapsulated suit. "D" level was civilian clothing. Only very responsible people could work in HazMat because you had to always be alert and watching out for each of your team members. Were the suits zipped up and masks working properly? Do we have the equipment and tools needed for the job?

We went to Florida and trained with Safety Systems using flammable liquids. This was a lot of fun except when we had to run the alligators out of the burn pits. We also did mutual aid to surrounding counties.

We had good men and women on this team, and we all worked well together.

The University of Louisville needed instructors to teach industrial businesses and fire and police departments. As a HazMat tech, I applied along with a few others from our department. As a result, I taught at the University of Louisville, Shelby Campus, for about six years until they lost their contract, which was through the University of Cincinnati and the Midwest Consortium. This teaching experience was great, and I enjoyed every minute of it. I guess it's because we learned while having fun. People who have been in some of my classes will tell you they usually had a good time. I still see some of those people occasionally and they will tell me one of my jokes or remind me of something funny that happened. Once when I was teaching a class at the University of Louisville, one of the men in the class fell asleep after lunch. I told Joe to wake John up, and Joe said, "You wake him up. You put him to sleep." This would wake them all up for a while.

Occasionally I would ask a new guy in class what does "t-o" spell. He would answer correctly. Then I asked what does "t-w-o" spell. Again, he answered correctly. Then I asked what does "t-w-a-i-n" spell, and he would say it correctly. Next, I would say, "Now put them together," and he would say, "to too twain." Then I'd say, "Keep practicing that, and tomorrow I will teach you to spell "lo-co-mo-tive." It always got a laugh and was a great icebreaker.

I also worked occasionally with a private company out of Indiana. We went to Alabama, Northern Kentucky, and Indiana to teach. The owner was a terrific lady whom I had met and worked with at the University of Louisville. We got along great and thought alike most of the time. Lee went with us and took pictures of the training so the boss could show the trainees if they were doing something the wrong way.

I was stationed at several different fire stations during my twenty-six-year career. I retired as a Hazardous Material Captain at Station 10 at Georgetown Street and New Circle Road. I served on Aerial 3 as a lieutenant and was later transferred to Engine 10 when it became a Haz-Mat (Hazardous Materials) Unit.

In 1995 Dr. Sartini at the Lexington Clinic put a stent in my heart. I was one of the first stent implant patients in Lexington. (Since then,

I have had several stents and a five-by-pass surgery.) Having the stent required that I retire or take disability from the Fire Department. I retired as a Hazardous Materials Captain in 1995. Today, if you get a stent, you go right back working where you were; but at that time if you had a heart or lung issue you were out of there.

I loved my career with the Lexington Fire Department and looked forward to going to work every day because you never knew what you were going to face. Lee was used to having every third night to herself. She didn't need to cook or do anything concerning me. When I retired, she said that I should rent my bed in the firehouse for a little while just in case she couldn't stand my being home every night. I think she eventually got used to it, although she had to give up her "me" night.

We had problems with our police and fire pensions over the years and still have issues to this day. The city did not fund our retirement at all. All the money in there is just what we put in plus the dividends from investments. Well, it seemed as though the city was always trying to take over that pension and put it in their treasury. We have had people in Frankfort for years trying to keep this from happening. Most police and fire personnel did not know Kentucky Senator Albert Robinson from Laurel County. He was my wife's brother-in-law. He worked diligently for our benefits, and that support for us is still beneficial today.

In the early years when a firefighter died, the widow was left virtually without financial assistance. When I came onto the department in 1969, our retirement fund was worth about $8 million. Now, it is worth somewhere over $1 billion. Widows at that time were getting about $100 month. Some were drawing $79 month. This was shameful, so our police and fire representatives got together with our lawyer and went to Frankfort to see what we could do to remedy the situation. Well, the Lexington mayor also had people in Frankfort who were sent to counter our plan.

Now, here's what happened. The mayor's people sat on one side of the room, and we sat on the other. There was a committee of about ten senators with my brother-in-law, Albert Robinson, as the chairman. As he called the meeting to order, he said he would like to introduce his sister-in-law and her husband. As we stood up to be recognized, the other side of the room literally hung their heads and melted into their chairs because they knew they had been had. Thank you, Senator Robinson, because at the end of the meeting, they voted 100 percent for LFUCG in Lexington to fix the situation or Frankfort would fix it for them with less favorable results for the city. A short time later the widows started getting $700 per month, then $1,000 per month, and now I think they get about $1,300 per month as a minimum.

PART 5
Fayette County Sheriff's Department

Transporting Prisoners
Juvenile Court
Game Warden Work

Wilbur teaching Safety and Security Class at church.

W hen I retired from the Fire Department in February, 1995, I trained for employment as a deputy with the Fayette County Sheriff Department. I was in training for about three months, and I loved every minute of it. We took a mandatory and very beneficial forty-hour in-service at Eastern Kentucky University every year. It kept us up to date on procedures, laws, and driver training, etc.

One of my classmates at the Sheriff's Department was Col. Richard Allen who had been a friend and deer hunting companion for years. The reason I call him Colonel is because he was an Air Force B-52 pilot in Vietnam where he flew over 200 missions. He was also a B-52 trainer for the pilots. After he retired, he was the Air Force Junior ROTC Commander at Bryan Station High School in Lexington for several years. Sometimes he would use Jess Craig, Gary Hicks, and me to help train his ROTC students in survivor camps.

Lt. Col. Allen was my partner in a lot of our training exercises at the Sheriff's Office. When we did our defense training, we put on proper padding for protection and beat on each other with our nightsticks--on the ground, on our knees, and standing up. As we were fighting one time, my nightstick—or baton as some call it--hit Allen on his thumb. It injured his thumb, but he kept right on fighting; and I didn't know he was hurt until the class was over. He was one tough deputy.

I don't know why, but when we had to spray each other with mace I asked if I could spray Col. Allen. They said it would be okay. I don't know who sprayed me, but Allen should have because of the way I treated him. We had to spray each other square in the face with the mace; it really hurt. The only relief was spray from a garden hose or sticking your head in a five-gallon bucket of water for about 45 minutes--not all at one time, we had to take turns. There was only one hose and one bucket for about thirty deputies. We fought over the hose and bucket.

We also did a lot of classroom training and lots of scenarios outside and inside our cruisers. One of our scenarios was at a traffic stop with two people in the vehicle. I was so focused on the two people in the car that I did not notice that another player had joined the scenario. He was behind me and out of sight behind a dumpster. Suddenly, he came out and shot me in the back. It was to teach us to be aware of our surroundings.

There were about thirty deputies in our class; and when the grades for all the training were turned in, I was number four on the list!

As Deputy Sheriff I served papers, made a few arrests, made a foot chase, and served as a bailiff in the court. I did not like being a bailiff, but it was a great experience. Col. Allen and I were partners on a lot of extraditions and were very safe, yet we made them very interesting.

Once I made an extradition out of Indianapolis, Indiana. When I asked the man what he was in for, he said he was making big money. "Well," I said, "that's a good thing. Everybody wants to make big money." He said it was a quarter inch too big. They caught him with a trunk full of it. This is a true story.

One day I was assigned to divorce court for eight hours, and it was the most miserable day of my life. I don't remember the female judge's name, but she was great. The people who came before her were mean, angry, liars, and you name it. One couple was seeking a divorce because he had attacked her and beat her up. Come to find out, they had pictures of the assault. She was a very large woman, and he was a small man; and apparently, she had attacked him instead. These kinds of things I listened to for eight hours. When court was over, I stepped over to the judge and told her I was going home to hug my wife and tell her I love her. I did just that, too.

My favorite job as deputy sheriff was transporting prisoners, and some of them told me they were glad I transported them. One man gave his heart to the Lord in the back of my cruiser as I transported him.

Another time a woman "trustee" was sitting on the back steps as I went inside the courthouse. She asked me how to be saved. I told her she needed to give her heart to the Lord, and she said, "Okay." I started with my speech about how to be saved and quoted scriptures. She said, "Can you hurry? My time is almost up, and I have to call my mom." So, forget quoting scriptures and formality. I immediately led her to Jesus while she sat on those steps. She said, "Thank you"; I left and never saw her again. I was never ashamed or too proud to share Jesus with others. Until you have led someone to Christ you don't know the joy of being a Christian.

I had a few incidents that I don't need to mention, but I want to tell you a story about a man about 50 years old who was in jail because his kids had drugs in his house. I had to go get him from another county jail and bring him to Fayette County for a court appearance. When I picked him up, he had a gallon Ziploc bag full of medicine with him. I brought that with him and checked it in with him to the Fayette County jail. Three days later I just happened to get the assignment of returning him to the jail where I had picked him up. When they brought him to me, he was a very sick man. He told me they would not give him any of his meds. As I was doing his paperwork, I asked for his meds; and they told me that when he came in, he didn't have any meds. I said, "Wait just a minute. I checked him in three days ago, and he had a bag of meds that I checked in with him." They were gone about ten minutes; and when they returned, they said they couldn't find it. I was beginning to get upset and indicated that I wanted to speak with the jailer. Again, they left; and in just a short time they returned with the man's meds. Now I don't want to say what I think was going on, but I do think I know. My prisoner was in a lot of pain in his stomach. I gave him his meds and bought him a hamburger on the way, and he was feeling much better by the time I got him back to the county where I had picked him up.

I transported all over the United States. If it was farther than 500 miles, we flew; and we always had two deputies on the trip. All out-of-state transports had two deputies regardless of distance, but in state we usually had only one deputy unless we were transporting females, in which case we always had a female deputy or female employee from the sheriff's office with us.

One of my favorite deputies who trained me on extraditions was Sydney Cranfield. We had crisscrossed this state to most counties and back. He and his wife adopted Lee and me, and we always enjoyed their company.

Sue Neff, Janice Price, and Dana Campbell accompanied me on many extraditions. Dana was so much fun to work with and we laughed a lot.

One time, Janice and I got our prisoner checked in early and arrived back to the airport in Kansas City where we had a long layover. Janice wasn't about to wait there, so she talked to someone, and we were out of there in short order. As we were checking in to board the plane in Kansas City, we went through the metal detector. I had put my Glock in my carry-on since we were not transporting a prisoner. The metal detector did not pick up the gun, and I began to think I had forgotten it in the rental car. I asked the inspectors to open the bag, and it was in there. It was hidden from the scanner by the metal strip running down the luggage.

Sue Neff is an artist, and she looks like she could be the twin of my sister Emma. We got them together once, and Sue painted a picture just for Sis. That was so special. All of us worked so well together. I still miss them.

One time I was on an extradition to Dayton, Ohio. After I picked up the prisoner, I got a call that I needed to pick up another one in Cincinnati. When I got to the jail in Cincinnati, I could not leave the first prisoner in the car by himself; so, I had to take him in and lock him up until I got the paperwork done to get the second one released to me. When I took him in, the guards helped me put him in a holding cell. As we approached the cell, a young man behind the bars started singing the song "Bad Boys, Bad Boys, What You Gonna Do When They Come for You" from a TV show. He sang that complete song word for word and ended with the credits about cops being filmed on location with men and women of law enforcement. When he finished, we all clapped for him because he did a great job; and I was impressed.

Another time I picked up a prisoner in Newport, Kentucky. He was a young man and had problems I was not aware of. He was about 25 years old but had been in a lot of trouble. He had 29 charges against him which required me to fill out a lot of paperwork. There were eight citations (pages) because four charges are all you can get on each citation. I had no problem doing this because this is just what you do all the time as part of the job. The man sat across the table from me as I did all this paperwork. I looked up at him and told him that if I had a rubber hose, I would beat him with it for making me do all this paperwork. I thought it was a good joke, but he started crying. Then I had to apologize and try to calm him down. It ended okay, but I learned that in the future I must be careful not to offend or stress someone.

One night I came out of Nicholasville with three prisoners in my car. It was just beginning to get dark, and my headlights went out, so I had to drive carefully on the way to the jail.

That reminds me of a story about Deputy Ed Haddix. He was riding his police bike and pulled up beside a lady who did not have her lights on as the sun was going down. Haddix had her roll down her window and advised her to turn her lights on. She looked at him strangely and told him to take his sunglasses off. Even the police need to be corrected sometimes.

While at the Sheriff's Office, I helped serve as Range Officer under the tutelage of Chief Lloyd Johnson. He helped get a grill installed for cooking our meals while we were training there. Our graduating class bought this grill, and I put a plaque on it to identify it. I had a lot of fun helping the deputies shoot better and qualify. I let my wife, Lee, use my Glock 17 to shoot the course, and she did so well I don't ever back-talk her.

During my years as a Deputy Sheriff, I had some awesome experiences--some funny, some serious. Hopefully you can easily tell the ones that are true or almost true or partly true.

The prosecutor was questioning a man who had witnessed a robbery on a very dark night. So, the prosecutor wanted to know how far he could see in the dark. After a short hesitation, the man said, "Well, I'm not sure, but I can see the moon." The prosecutor said," No more questions, your Honor."

One day a 14-year-old male came to court with his pants sagging way down under his buttocks showing a lot of skin, and the female judge told him to pull them up. He said he couldn't pull them up. I think he got the message when the judge looked over at me. I didn't like his attitude anyway and was hoping she would tell me to put him in the holding cell till he got his pants up. He could see where this was going, so he pulled them up. The judge told him to never again come back into her court looking like that.

I transported a lot of juveniles to Juvenile facilities all over Kentucky. It was always a joy to see the staff at these places get their attention when I delivered them. When some of these kids got there, they were sullen, belligerent, and incorrigible; but before I left them, they were saying, "yes sir, no sir, yes ma'am, no ma'am!" I always went back to my car smiling. I knew they were going to get help there. I believe when they came home, some were different young people.

What really bothered me was to see these young people have no respect for themselves or anyone else. Many of them were already using drugs, too. And that reminds me of a poem that was published in the Paintsville Herald News, Paintsville, Kentucky, several years ago. It is called "Meet Mr. & Mrs. Crystal Meth" by 21-year-old Alicia Von Davis. It was found on her body.

I destroy homes, I tear families apart
I take your children and that's just the start.
I'm more valued than diamonds, more precious than gold.
The sorrow I bring is a sight to behold.
If you need me, remember, I'm easily found
I live all around you, in school and in town.
I live with the rich; I live with the poor,
I live just down the street and maybe next door.
I am made in a lab, but not like you think:
I can be made under a kitchen sink,
In your child's closet, or even out in the woods.
If this scares you to death, then it certainly should.
I have many names, but there's one you'll know best.
I'm sure you've heard of me. My name is Crystal Meth.
My power is awesome, try me, you'll see;
But if you do, you may never break free.
Just try me once and I might let you go.
But if you try me twice, then I'll own your soul.
When I possess you, you'll steal, and you'll lie.
You'll do what you have to do, just to get high.
The crimes you'll commit for my narcotic charms
Will be worth the pleasures you feel in my arms.
You'll lie to your mother; you'll steal from your dad.
When you see their tears, you must feel sad.
Just forget your morals and how you were raised.
I'll be your conscience, I'll teach you my ways.

I take kids from their parents; I take parents from their kids.
I turn people from God. I separate friends.
I'll take everything from you, your looks, and your pride.
I'll be with you always, right by your side.
You'll give up everything, your family, your home,
Your money, your true friend; then you'll be alone.
I'll take and take 'til you have no more to give.
When I finish with you, you'll be lucky to live.
If you try me, be warned: this is not a game.
If I'm given the chance, I'll drive you insane.
I'll ravage your body; I'll control your mind,
I'll own you completely, your soul will be mine.
The nightmares I'll give you when you're lying in bed,
And the voices you'll hear from inside your head,
The sweats, the shakes, and the visions you'll see.
I want you to know these things are gifts from me.
By then it's too late, and you'll know in your heart
That you are now mine; and we shall not part.
You'll regret that you tried me (they always do),
But you came to me, not I to you.
You knew this would happen, many times you were told.
But you challenged my power, you chose to be bold.
You could have said no, and then walked away.
If you could live that day over now, what would you say?
My power is awesome, as I told you before.
I can take your life and make it so dim and sore.
I'll be your master and you'll be my slave.
I'll even go with you when you go to your grave.
Now that you've met me, what will you do?
Will you try me or not? It's all up to you.
I can show you more misery than words can tell.
Come take my hand, let me lead you to HELL.

I came to know the State Game Warden in a neighboring county
and rode with him twice. One time we got a call from someone stating
that there were some coon hunters on the back of his property, so we

went to check it out. We parked about a half mile away and started out on foot in the dark. We could see and hear them from that distance. As we approached, I stayed quiet and walked behind this giant of a man. The young boys with the men had flashlights and were making lots of noise so they did not hear us coming. We walked within 15 feet of the group, and the Game Warden said, "What are you guys doing?" They almost jumped out of their skin! They had come from Corbin to hunt but failed to get permission to hunt on this man's farm. Now this Game Warden is a kind-hearted man and did not take their guns or punish them in any way but sent them home with a warning. I imagine they were thankful all the way home. It could have ended a lot differently for them. Illegal hunting of any kind is a serious offense in Kentucky. They had young boys with them, and the Warden thought this was the best way to handle the situation.

Another time the Game Warden got a call to go down to a campground where some people were on a hayride and having a good old time. Those folks had hired a man to drive the tractor and pull the wagon while they got drunk, but the problem was that the tractor driver had gotten drunk also. Now, another problem was that they had all parked about five miles away at a church. So, how do you get that wagon load of people and the driver back to their vehicles? I ended up driving the tractor with the wagon. Since the night was cold, I wore the Warden's huge jacket to keep from freezing. He arrested the tractor driver for DUI, and we took him to jail. The others must have made it home because we had no accidents that night. As Captain Stivers, who was a legend at the firehouse used to say, "And a good time was had by all."

Most of the time prisoners are not a problem for deputies, but sometimes they can get a little rowdy. Another deputy and I were transporting two men to KCPC for evaluation to determine if they were competent to stand trial. One of the men turned around in his seatbelt and began furiously kicking the other man. He had kicked him in the face before I could get stopped and get him out of the car. I'm glad we were in the other deputy's car because we had blood to clean up. We called our Lexington office, and they sent another unit to our location just west of Frankfort. We transported the men in separate vehicles, and we were glad to get rid of those guys.

I thoroughly enjoyed working at the Sheriff's Department. They are a special bunch of people, and I have lots of friends there.

Everyone knew how much I enjoyed transporting prisoners, but my last eight months as Deputy Sheriff I was assigned to Juvenile Court, which I hated and asked not to be assigned to. These juveniles have no respect for anyone or for the laws. They spit on you, run, fight, or whatever and always yelling obscenities. We were not allowed to shackle (leg chains) them, which I thought would have been a good lesson for them. I asked repeatedly to be reassigned, but it seemed no one heard me. So, I turned in my cruiser and all my equipment and left the Sheriff's Department after ten years of service.

PART 6
Civilian Life

Family Member Kidnapped
Part-Time Jobs
Hobbies
Volunteer Work

JUST GOT MY CONNIE
HOME FROM HOSPITAL

Glenn and Connie
Bays Wedding

Rafting New River, WV

LOVE
THIS
FLAG

IT REALLY DID GO
THROUGH THERE!!
ATLANTA

GRANDSON JOHN

Ziplining Branson, MO 2016

CHIEF
WHITECLOUD

Will the real Sam Clark please stand up!!
Sam Clark, Bill Breeze, Wilbur

DERRICK   AUSTIN & JAMIE

THE MEDLEYS

GREAT GRANDSON
AUSTIN
THE HUNTER

MAMMAW MORGAN
LOVED ME BEFORE
LEE DID.

AUSTIN AND PAPAW

BAYS CLAN -
GLENN, MARIE, CONNIE, ADIE, MEGAN, JOE & MOLLY

In the early 70s, Lee's mother and her uncles, Ben, and Berry Bowles, had a piece of property in the Daniel Boone Forest near S-Tree Tower Recreational Area in Jackson County, near McKee, Kentucky. They priced the property, and we paid their price. On the property was an old cabin which was built in 1923 when this area was being logged for timber by their father, Tom Bowles. Some of these rough-cut boards were 14-15 inches wide and over one inch thick. Talk about heavy!

Several of my friends and family helped me tear this building down. Carl Travis, Jim Goodlett, Wilbert Lemay, my pastor Dave Allen, and Wiley "Buck" Isaacs from Sand Gap went with us at various times to demolish the old cabin and build the new cabin with a new chimney. We used all the old oak boards in our new cabin. They were so hard we could barely get nails in them. The new cabin was 23 feet long and 13 feet wide. It had two rooms with a fireplace at one end and the kitchen at the other end. I also built a porch eight feet wide the whole length of the cabin, and it had four cedar posts for pillars. We sat out there and looked out over the Daniel Boone Trail, now called the Sheltowee Trace. That was the name given to Boone by Chief Blackfish when he was captured and taken to Detroit. The trail runs near our farm. I loved to sit on the porch and watch it snow across the field and the winding creek with a field, a barn, and hills on the far side of the creek. We spent several nights in our cabin and cooked some good meals.

The problem was that the property was four miles from the nearest highway, and the road was not that great. As a matter of fact, we nearly got stuck a few times in our 4 x 4 truck pulling a trailer with our building supplies. We had to cross the creek to get to our place; and, at that time, the crossing was extremely rough. I can tell some funny stories about that place.

One true story is the time we got the truck stuck coming up out of the creek onto the road on the other side. It would not go forward or backward as it had slid sideways into a rut. I attached a winch cable to the rear hitch; and my mother-in-law, Ethel Morgan, waded the creek to attach the other end of the cable to a small sapling on the bank. With Lee in the driver's seat, me prying from the front with a large wooden pole that I had cut, and Mamaw on the winch cable, we maneuvered the truck backward into the creek to get a better run at the bank. I waded in and unhooked the cable and got into the driver's seat, and we hit that bank with mud flying and came up out of there. Lee's four-year-old niece, Amanda, was in the truck with us; and with eyes big as saucers, she told everyone that Mamaw pulled the truck out of the creek! That is the way she saw it, and 40 years later she is sticking to it!!

The cabin was broken into several times. One time a London policeman and his son camped there for several days and burned up all our wood that we had cut. He had broken out a window to get in. We knew this because the Gilberts who lived out on Route 1955 had a lot of land down there that they farmed, and Herman Gilbert told us about them.

Another time, a man from Cincinnati called us and asked if he could take his family there. They were very nice people and stayed for quite a while. He even made improvements (like putting iron shutters on the windows), and always left it clean. They came down nearly every weekend. He always checked to see if we were going first.

One time, someone broke in and took all our supplies and dumped them in the middle of the floor and ground it in with their feet. Then they took all six hurricane lamps off the walls, took them to the creek, and smashed them on the rocks. Why? We also had a wonderful old "Warm Morning" stove in the living room. They stole it and the stove pipes! We did everything possible to protect our place, and the sad part is that we had just recently canceled the insurance on it.

In 1988 I had gone to Missouri to a Royal Ranger Camporama, and Lee got a phone call from one of the Gilberts who owned about 700 acres around there. Herman was working in the fields and saw someone at the cabin. He went to investigate and found that two queers had broken in and were staying there. They were mad at each other and were fighting; one of them started walking down the road with his backpack. The other man said he was going to kill him. Then he changed his mind and said he was going to burn his cabin. Not believing he would, Herman went back to work in the fields and looked up to see smoke at the cabin. Sure enough, he did burn it. The state police said that unless you have an eyewitness, even with a confession, nothing can be done about it. We never built it back, but we still have the property.

We have had such a full and interesting life.

Now in every family a little rain must fall, and it was no different in ours. Life is not always fair, and we don't understand, but we know that trials make us stronger if we get through them.

My wife's sister, Kay was kidnapped many years ago and went through several days of fear and torture. She worked at night and carpooled with a friend. When she did not show at the parking lot to ride to work, the friend called her mother the next morning to inquire if Kay was sick. Mother informed her that Kay had, in fact, left for work on time the night before. They immediately informed the authorities and law enforcement of her disappearance. In just a few hours they determined that her car was hidden behind the church where she always left it until she came back the next morning after work. Her car was unlocked with her purse in it, and one of her shoes was found in the parking lot. They could tell there had been a struggle. That same day an APB was issued.

Senator Albert Robinson, her brother-in-law, was also involved in the search; and this helped the family in many ways. Finally, a call came from the FBI that she had been found alive and would be arriving at the Cincinnati airport where we should pick her up. They let her talk on the phone to her mom and daughter, and they all cried. So, we all piled into our van and drove to the airport.

On the drive home, she shared with us what had happened.

The kidnapper had parked his car in the same location where she always parked when meeting her ride. He had hidden it behind the church building out of sight of the road and front parking lot. He walked through the woods and pastures to get to her house. There, he got into her car and lay down in the back floorboard and waited for her to get into the car and drive away from the house. When he felt they were far enough away from the house, he raised up out of the back floorboard and put his hand over her face. She started screaming, and he threatened her with a huge flashlight. She tried to get out, but the doors were automatically locked and had to be opened manually. He kept struggling to keep her quiet and jumped over the front seat and started wrestling with her. Finally, he wrestled her down on the seat, sat on her, and drove to the church where he parked beside his car. He forced her out of the car and attempted to handcuff her. She fought furiously and ran toward the road, but he dragged her back each time. No cars ever came by for her to flag. They fought on the ground for a long time. He finally got his knees on her chest; she was exhausted. (At some point, she lost a shoe in the struggle, which was a good thing, since it was a clue for law enforcement.) He then commenced to get her into the back seat of his car with the child locks on. She resisted for a long while, and each time he tried to shut the doors she would kick them open. Finally, he succeeded and put handcuffs on her with her hands in the front of her and drove away. He remained mostly quiet at this time. When they got on I-75 South, she could only imagine where they were headed. She held her hands up for every vehicle that passed, but no one saw her. Apparently, it was too dark inside the car. He realized what she was doing and insisted she lie down and continued threatening her with the long-handled Mag light. It would have done serious damage or even may have killed her if he used it, so she decided to be still. Then he pulled onto a country road and tried to put a second pair of handcuffs on her ankles, but they would not fit; therefore, he handcuffed her hands behind her back. She lay down and quietly prayed and eventually slept. Later in the night they stopped for gas, and he threw a quilt over her and warned her not to sit up. They got back on the road but sometime later they stopped, and he loosened the handcuffs because she was badly bruised by then.

In Arkansas, they stopped at a motel. While he was inside registering, she was locked in the car with a quilt over her. He locked all the doors and took the key. She could not unlock any of the doors without the engine running. He then drove around to the back of the motel where their room was located. He took her out of the car and draped the quilt around her back, but she straightened up so that the quilt fell off. There she stood in handcuffs and barefoot, but no one was around to see. It was early in the morning by this time, and dawn was approaching.

Once inside the room, he barricaded the door with a rollaway bed and a dresser. Next, he took the bathroom door off the hinges and hid the phone so she couldn't get to it. All this time he was armed with a pistol.

He took her into the bathroom and forced her to shower with him. Once they were out of the shower, he raped her. He then cried and apologized and said he would put her on a plane in the morning to send her home. But when he awoke, he was not apologetic. It seemed he was schizophrenic and once again became the monster. They got in the car and headed west, and he told her she would never see her family again. He was going to chain her to a cactus to dry up like dry bones.

At some point, he pulled off the road and changed her handcuffs to the front in her lap. Later, he stopped on a very rural road; and she assumed this was where she would die. Instead, he placed each hand in separate handcuffs and hooked them to the same door handle. He left them very loose. She was bruising so badly. Sometime later she realized she could slip her hands out of the cuffs and prayed for an opportunity to escape.

He stopped for fuel. She had her hands out of the cuffs waiting for the opportunity to escape; but, as usual, he turned the engine off and took the key after locking the doors. He got back into the car and pulled in the front of the station where there was a grocery. He stopped the car and got out leaving the car running and went inside for some reason. She jumped over the front seat and hit the door locks as she saw his hand on the car. She floored it while holding the horn down and almost hit a car backing out of a parking space. She headed east on I-40 driving about 90 mph. In just a few minutes she found the Arkansas State Police Barracks, parked, and ran inside. (The State Police there were on the phone with the local police department in Oklahoma where she had just fled from.) Her abductor had reported the car stolen so the locals and state police were looking for the car. When she walked into the police barracks, the state patrolman told them the car had just pulled into their parking lot. Here she stands, bare foot and wrists bruised. She told them about the gun, the flashlight, and the handcuffs, and that she had been kidnapped and had escaped. They went to the car and found everything just as she told them. They called back to the local Oklahoma police department and told them to arrest him and not to release him until the Kentucky State Police advised them what to do with him.

A sheriff's deputy from Oklahoma showed up about five minutes after she reached the Arkansas State Police and said he was on the way to find her when he had gotten the call of a stolen car.

She was very shaken and sick with fatigue, but she felt safe and secure with the Arkansas State Police staff. She called her mother and daughter, and they talked a couple of times. Someone brought her fried chicken for supper. The FBI was called in since it was an interstate crime, and an FBI officer went to Walmart and bought her a pair of shoes since she had lost hers. They were too small, but she didn't care at that point. He took her to the airport and called home to give the family details on the flight. The FBI officer bought her ticket. When the clerk at the counter asked for her identification, she had none because her purse was left in her car when she was kidnapped. The FBI officer showed the clerk his badge and said, "She is who she says she is." Kay felt comforted again when the clerk said, "That's good enough for me."

Approximately 72 hours elapsed from the time she was kidnapped until we met her in Cincinnati, but it felt like an eternity. When we pulled into the terminal area to pick her up, we all just broke down. There she stood—barefoot, carrying her too-small shoes, with no coat or purse, looking so pitiful. We were all so relieved. As we made our way back home, she gave an account of her harrowing experience and gave us permission to record her telling us what had occurred. For the most part, we just let her talk as we all prayed silently, thanking God that she was safe and heading back home with us. Our brother-in-law, Senator Albert Robinson, prayed a prayer of thanksgiving over her when we were all back home together.

Although we all have problems in this life, there are more things that are good and wonderful that happen to us. A few years ago, my wife, Lee, and I went to Washington, D.C., with our daughter, Connie, and her husband, Glenn. We saw a lot of things and had a wonderful time, but the most memorable part for me was when we visited Mt. Vernon, George Washington's Homestead. This is also where he is buried, and we got to visit his tomb. At 10 a.m. and 2 p.m. each day there is a memorial service, complete with placing a wreath at his tomb. Everyone who participates gets to sign the book, and it was such a privilege for me to be included.

The hostess in charge of the ceremony had five military volunteers come up for the special ceremony with a prayer before placing the wreath at the tomb. When I walked up, the ceremony was about to begin; and I asked if I could participate. The lady said she had all she needed and that she usually used military personnel or veterans. She asked me if I was one, and I said that I was. One of the men whom she had selected said he was not military, and he gave up his position in the ceremony for me. I couldn't thank him enough because I was so humbled by this. A prayer was said by one of the other men, and I got to place the wreath which was a huge honor for me. Then we signed the official book, and I signed it like John Hancock--REALLY BIG! You may not understand this, but I think we all had a tear or two. It was a big deal for us. Oh, how I long for a leader like George Washington, and I believe President Trump is as close as we will come to having one.

Paul Mitchell was another man I loved and thought a lot of. He was a captain on the Lexington Fire Department and a sergeant on the Fayette County Sheriff's Department. Paul was a talented man and one of a kind. He was an expert in karate, electronics, communications, knife making, reloading ammo, and gunsmith. He built an AR-15 rifle for me to use in a special class for a boys' program. I cleaned it; and when I handed it to him for inspection, he said, "If it's clean enough for you, it's clean enough for me." Then he said, "It's yours, keep it." That's the kind of person he was.

He was also a pilot and took me flying many times in his private plane. We flew all over the state and had lots of fun. One time we were flying low over our farm in Jackson County, and I said, "Paul, you better get up out of here because there are cliffs up here." He very calmly said, "I'm trying." He even let me fly the plane and taught me how to stay level, turn, dive, and climb. He let me do what they call a "stall" where you climb straight up as far as possible, and then the plane starts sliding backward. Since the motor is heavier than the back, the nose comes around and starts to dive and goes into a spin. You don't want to do that close to the ground. That's when Paul took the controls and pulled us out of it.

When I decided to put an air conditioner in my old camper, which I still use, he rewired it for me. He also rewired my utility trailer and my garage door. Oh yeah, and he had to rewire my old pickup truck to get my trailer lights to work! What a guy he was.

Paul was a very private person. When he was in the hospital dying, I didn't even know it until he was buried. I felt so bad about that. I do hope I will see him again someday, and I am so glad I could call him my friend and brother. I still miss him very much.

After I had been on the Fire Department for about a year, I decided to go to Lexington Barber College on High Street. Bill Diamond was our instructor. Since I was at the Fire Department every third day, it took me thirteen months to do a nine-month course. I graduated fourth in my class of about thirty. When I was in the Marines on the ship, I cut the men's hair with non-electric, old-fashioned hand clippers so I had a good start. This was good exercise for my hands.

While we were in training at barber school, the students who had been there the longest and were the best trained had the chairs closest to the entrance door and the less trained were toward the back of the shop. There was a man who was not very clean and lived on the street. From time to time, he would come in to get a shave and a haircut. Since I was a new student and was on the very back seat, I did not know what was happening. There I stood with this man after everyone else disappeared. What could I do? Since I am hardly ever lost for words, I looked at that man and said, "Get up here in my chair; I used to scrape hogs." He smiled and jumped in my chair, and I did a really good job on him. I don't know if I could get away with joking like that these days. I'd probably get "expelled" from barber school.

I learned all kinds of things on my journey to the front of the shop. I learned how to put butch wax on the earpiece of the shop phone and then go call that number and have a new student answer it. The new student didn't know there was a problem till he got no answer and removed the phone from his ear and heard the popping from the sticky earpiece. Oh, how mean we were; but it was so much fun.

I don't want to give up all our secrets, but I must share this with you. It seemed that no matter how much we practiced getting a straight razor sharp, it almost never happened; but we did keep trying. We all had razor straps that hung on the side of our chairs. So, we practiced like we saw in the old westerns. At some point in the move, we had to flip the knife over and go in the opposite direction. Inevitably we missed a turn and cut a gash in the strap. We then used our neighbor's strap! But it didn't matter because in the end everyone's strap had gashes! Since we could never seem to get our straight razors sharp enough, we had a little trick we did. We had razors that used replacement blades. When we did a shave, we placed a warm towel over the eyes of the customer while we shaved him. We proceeded with the fourteen steps to complete the shave; and when we finished the shave, we put the folding razor away. With the straight razor in hand, we removed the towel from his eyes; and the customer was happy with a good shave.

When I finished barber school, I went to work with Lonnie Cope at his shop on Walnut Street next to the phone company building across from City Hall. Lonnie loved a good joke, and sometimes we would have all of City Hall standing at the windows being entertained. Sometimes watching the spectators was as funny as watching the ones being pranked. One time, Lonnie tied a wallet to a string which he ran through a crack in the sidewalk and secured it to something so that it could not be broken loose. Then he laid the wallet by the curb and watched the people as they walked by. Whatever you think happened, well it did. It was so funny to watch their reactions when they realized they had been tricked. Another prank he played was gluing coins to the sidewalk.

A black man named Huckle Buck was our shoeshine man. He did a really good job shining shoes, and we all loved him. Lonnie loved pulling tricks on him when he would doze in his chair from time to time. One day when he went to sleep in the chair, his head leaned back. And somehow a string was placed around his neck. Lonnie hollered "shoeshine," and Huckle Buck nearly strangled getting out of that chair so fast. He was a good sport, and we all had tricks played on us.

Haircuts cost $3.25 back then. One day a man who wanted a shave and a haircut came in, so I proceeded with all the things I had learned in barber school. While shaving him, I cut a nick or two. To stop the bleeding, I tore a small piece of paper from the neck wrap paper and stuck it on the nicks, like Floyd, the barber, did on Andy Griffith. When I finished, the guy paid me, plus he gave me a $10 tip. I said "Man, that's a great tip. Are you sure?" He said, "Yes. I believe in paying a man for what he's worth--a barber, a butcher, and a paper hanger all at the same time." I don't think I ever saw him again, and I believe Lonnie lost that customer.

Lee and I have always been involved in church. Of course, Daddy Brown was a preacher, and we were always involved in church activities.

Daddy Brown took us to a church where he was speaking, and we were expected to testify or sing. Lee's family was always active in church as well.

When I got out of the Marines and came to Lexington, Lee and I started attending church here. First, we went to the Church of God on Wilderness Road, then to Trinity Pentecostal where all the Chrismans (Lee's distant cousins who worked at the Fire Department) attended, and then to First Assembly of God on Clays Mill Road for a couple of years. In the 1970s, a church was being built close to where we lived on the north side of town. Every day as we drove by, we watched as it was being built. When it was completed, we started attending there. It was called Faith Assembly of God with Ed Jones as pastor. After seeing him make some very difficult decisions, I prayed that the Lord would never call me to be a pastor. Someone said I was cut out to be a preacher, but they sewed me up wrong.

One time we went forward to pray for someone who was sick, and Brother Jones asked that only those who really believed in healing should come forward to pray for those who were seeking healing. I was very impressed with this. Many times, I went to him for advice, and sometimes he would laugh at my lack of knowledge. I even thought it was funny after he explained it to me. Once I went into his office and told him I found a contradiction in the Bible when I was studying for a Royal Rangers meeting. The catching away of the church could happen at any time and that's when Christ returns for those who are looking for Him. This is not the Second Coming. Then in Revelation 1:7, when Christ returns to earth after the Rapture, that is the Second Coming, and every eye shall see Him. Brother Jones straightened me out on this matter. We got involved at Faith Assembly of God, and we never looked back. I worked in the sound booth and served as Sunday School Superintendent. A few years later we built a new facility on Kingston Road in Lexington. This was so exciting. We were very involved in every step of the building process. I helped attach the beams and the steeple as I hung in a sling from a lift.

Several pastors have had a great influence on our lives, and we loved them all. After Ed Jones retired, Brother Hutchison came; then came Brother Collier and his wife Anita and their two sons, David, and Chris.

The Colliers were called to the Missions and left to go to language school in Costa Rica. That's when Garroll Finch and Raegie came to Faith Assembly. Brother Finch helped us build our new facility on Kingston Road. Then Randy and Jennifer Weeks became our pastors. We made the decision to attend Bread of Life Church where our close friend, Dave Allen was pastor. We have been with Dave and Lynn all the years since my military days. He and Lynn have tremendously blessed us and are like family. Dave is a retired civil engineer and a licensed geologist. He worked for the University of Kentucky while pastoring. He helped me build my cabin in Jackson County that I mentioned earlier.

In 1976, my sister, Emma, and her husband, Jim Goodlett, built a skating rink on Lancaster Road in Richmond, Kentucky. He asked my brother-in-law, Wilbert Lemay, and me to work as skate guards. We thought it would be fun, and we were not disappointed. Jim's four daughters worked the concessions, as did Lee and my sister, Joyce. Jim's older daughters became skate guards as did some of the nieces. He also had skate guards younger than Wilbert and me, but we all got along with all the skaters.

Jim has always been a businessman. He owned a nursing home in Richmond and knew how to make money whether doing these things, building houses to sell, or owning a recycle center.

In 1977, I started working with a boys' group called Royal Rangers which was started in 1962 by Johnnie Barnes. The National Assemblies of God Office in Springfield, Missouri, asked Johnnie to start a ministry for boys; and God gave him a dream of what it was going to look like. Johnnie built the program from the ground up. What a powerful ministry it has turned out to be all over the world, with Boy Scouts being the only boys' program in the world that is larger than Royal Rangers. This program is very similar to the Boy Scouts, but I think it is a lot better. We teach a good Christian curriculum, and we give the boys discipleship classes. Royal Rangers is the greatest program in the world for boys to learn about life: how to live, how to survive, how to take on responsibility, and how to live a Christian life and lead others to Christ. The reason Royal Rangers is so successful is that we understand that boys like three things: things that are big, loud, and unusual. "Royal" means belonging to a King (Jesus), and "Rangers" means action and adventure.

I worked with the Kentucky District Commander Orval James and became a Sectional Commander in the Bluegrass Section. In 1980, Commander James asked me to take over as Kentucky District (State) Commander, and I told him I was too busy. He just looked at me and said that was what he needed--someone who was busy. Busy people get things done. So, here we go, and for eight years I traveled the state working with other churches, organizing outposts, and teaching leader training sessions. I then turned the district leadership over to Tim Snyder who continued to grow the program.

While Lee was travelling all over the state and giving leader training sessions for the Girls Ministries, I was travelling for the Royal Rangers Program. Our daughter later said that all she ever heard was Royal Rangers and Missionettes. We always had papers scattered all over our living room floor and tables getting ready for the next events. I guess that is mostly true although we did a lot of family activities as well.

By attending training camps, I learned how to reach, teach, and keep boys for Christ. I worked with Commander Barnes and with our National Frontier Camping Fellowship coordinator, Fred Deaver. What a privilege it was because they were such men of God and leaders for His cause. They traveled all over the world to spread the Royal Ranger Program, and to date Royal Rangers is established in over 95 countries of the world.

Fred Deaver was a professional artist who has his artwork all over the world. I am privileged to have several of his prints in my home. He was commissioned to paint a portrait of John Wayne for the Boy Scouts. When he finished, Wayne was so pleased with it that he asked Fred what he could do for him. Fred asked John Wayne for that old sweaty hat he wore in all his western movies, but Wayne could not bring himself to part with it. I wonder who ended up with the hat.

Johnnie was also an artist, and I have one of his special paintings called "The Commander." I was at a National Training Conference in Indiana, and his painting was for sale. He wanted me to have it so badly that he picked up an old mattock out of my truck and said he needed it for his garden. He then gave me the painting in exchange. So, we were even; but I doubt that he needed that mattock.

One time Johnnie and Fred were in their impressive uniforms sitting in an airport. The uniform consists of gray slacks and a navy blazer with the epaulets with rank insignia pins and the gold and silver embroidered Royal Ranger emblem on the left chest. They were sharp looking. (Lee said she loves a man in uniform. I wore the Marine, Fire Department, Royal Ranger, and Sheriff Department uniforms. Maybe that's why we are still married!) A man kept looking at them and finally asked who they were. Without a beat, Johnnie said, "Have you ever heard of the Green Berets?", and he said he had. Then Johnnie asked him about the Navy Seals, and his response was affirmative. Then Johnnie said, "We train them." The man was impressed. Johnnie never told him differently. Actually, that was true. We have men from every walk of life in our organization working with our boys, and they are required to do lots of training. In my Royal Ranger National Training Camp at Camp McKee in Kentucky, I had men from many walks of life. Many are active and retired military. One was active CIA.

Commander Barnes had a saying that we all adopted as our own: "You never stand so tall as when you stoop to help a boy."

National Training Camp is four days of rigorous training where the outpost leaders become the boys in their outposts and learn the problems and difficulties of leading boys. The national staff who lead these camps treat these men as though they were young boys. This camp has evolved into NRMC, National Ranger Ministry Camp, and is very intense.

At a National Training Camp in Indiana, Commander Barnes was the Camp Commander and Fred Deaver was the Senior Guide. The Senior Guide is tough like a drill instructor in the military and was the man who kept the camp running and everything going smoothly. The trainers came in on Tuesday to get the camp ready for the event before the trainees came in on Thursday. One of the things to be done was to get the assembly area ready. This included putting up three flag poles. On Tuesday we set these poles up in what we thought was a beautiful spot. The next day, Commander Barnes wanted those poles moved to another location: three more holes dug and the flag poles moved.

Everything was fine until Thursday morning before the men arrived for the camp. When Commander Barnes got up that morning, he wanted the flags moved again. So here we go again. We dug three more holes and moved the flag poles. I guess it was a good thing, because I am going to tell you why Commander Barnes was such a good leader. This time, there was a lake behind the flag poles which the men would look at during morning devotions. This is when the geese came in. He waited until all the geese had landed on the lake, and then he continued with the devotions. What a leader!

Another time, Johnnie was flown to Louisville, Kentucky, to speak at the morning service in one of our Assembly of God churches. I was there on stage with them, as the Royal Ranger Kentucky District Commander. The pastor had so much stuff going on that morning including campaigning for someone in the church who was running for a local judge. Then he turned to Johnnie and told him he had five minutes to speak. I could not believe this was happening since they had spent money getting him there and motel and honorarium, etc. I checked my watch and when Johnnie finished, it was exactly five minutes to the second! What a man!

In 1989, the National Royal Ranger Department dedicated a full issue of the *High Adventure* magazine to the memory of Johnnie Barnes. I was asked to write a memorial for this issue, and it went like this:

"Johnnie Barnes was the humblest man I think I ever met. I could write until Jesus comes and still not express my love and respect for him. I first met Johnnie at the Men's Ministries conference in Dayton, Ohio. Even though I was thirty-some years old at the time, I know how every boy feels who meets this man's man.

It was the little things that Johnnie did that impressed me, such as pushing his paintings. He traded me one of his prints for an old, beat-up mattock that I had in my truck. He said he needed it to do some work around the house. Ha!

Another time at an NTC (National Training Camp) in Indiana, Johnnie was giving the morning devotion, and three geese flew directly over us. Johnnie saw them first because he was facing them, so he stopped his devotion and had the men watch until the geese were out of sight, then he continued his devotion.

Yes, we are going to miss Johnnie. But there's a song that says, "Look for Me for I Will Be There Too"; so, Commander Barnes, look for me, for I may not be able to recognize you for the brightness of the stars in your crown."

Johnnie Barnes went to Heaven in 1988, and the Royal Ranger Ministry lost a great leader.

I am still involved in the Royal Rangers' FCF (Frontier Camping Fellowship), a frontier program for boys ages eleven and older and men who want to get involved in a program that depicts the pre-1840s. We dress like the frontiersmen, live in teepees and lodges, shoot muzzleloaders, throw tomahawks and knives, cook over open fires that we start with flint and steel, and just have a great time. We encourage all the boys and men to take up a trade or hobby that fits that period. Mine is working with leather, making pouches and belts. I also make chokers like the old frontiersmen and Indians wore. These are made with glass beads, bone, leather, sinew, and other items for decorations.

The FCF Motto is "To Give and To Serve." We teach the boys to keep the spirit of FCF alive by achievement, courage, friendship, servant leadership, and woodsman crafts. We dress, camp, cook, and act like we were living in the pre-1840s.

I used to be a pretty good hawk and knife thrower, but it's amazing what some of these young boys can do. A few years ago, we were at a camp where there was a tree with a split in it about four inches wide. The boys set up a target on the other side of the tree, and I threw my throwing knife through the slit and stuck it perfectly in the target. I went to the target, pulled my knife out, put it in my belt sheath, and walked away! Later in the day there was no bark on that tree around that split and much of the tree itself was gone. The boys had so much fun throwing their hawks and knives through it.

Frontier Camping Fellowship (FCF) is a terrific program for men and boys. There is a lot of bonding, making memories, and Christian fellowship. It is character building at its very core. It is so relaxing to set up camp, put my buffalo skin over my chair, and sit around the campfire telling stories or singing songs, and just forget about all the troubles of this world. It's just so peaceful to sit in our old-time chairs and talk about all kinds of things. We take communion, pray, and rejoice around the campfire. At the end of the day, we sit around the campfire with the boys and have devotions and present the Word of God to them. Then, after this we may tell some tall tales—some true and some not-- that will keep their attention right up to the end of the story and bedtime.

One of the stories I like to tell is about a bear chasing me. When he was just about to grab me, I could feel his hot breath on my back. I knew what I was going to do, but the bear did not know my intentions. I stopped, turned around quickly, reached down his throat, grabbed his tail, and jerked hard. I turned that bear inside out. Now he was headed the other way, and I went in the opposite direction. We always have new boys and men, so the stories get told over and over.

The following is a favorite story I like to tell on a commander. We were on a campout in Eastern Kentucky and got lost in the woods. After a while, we got thirsty and tried to find some water to drink. We finally came up on this old house--or should I say shack--with a well in the yard. As the commander and I were approaching the well, an old lady came out of the house and walked toward us. She was not very clean but was very friendly and smiled showing a few rotten teeth. After seeing this, the commander and I tried to decide which side of the dipper she drank from so we could drink from the other side. Now he was quite clever and turned that dipper up on end and drank deeply from the end of that dipper opposite the handle. When he finished, she laughed and said that she had lived there nigh on fifty years and he was the only person other than she who had ever drunk from that dipper like that.

Another story I like to tell the boys is about a country where some of our missionaries go. That country is where they take an unborn embryo from an animal and eat it. Then they take strips off the belly of another animal and eat it. To wash it down they squeeze a liquid from the mammary glands of another animal and drink it. By this time the boys are gagging, spitting, and making all kinds of noises of rejection. This is when I tell them that they just ate that stuff for breakfast: eggs, bacon, and milk.

When a boy or man is initiated into FCF, he is taught how to make an Indian bead necklace which then belongs to him. Jess Craig teaches them how to build their own candle lanterns. These are items they receive at initiation.

Here is a poem by Alan Beck entitled "What Is a Boy?"

Between the innocence of babyhood and the dignity of manhood,
we find a delightful creature called a boy. Boys come in assorted
sizes, weights, and colors, but all boys have the same creed:

143

To enjoy every second of every minute of every hour of every day and to protest with noise (their only weapon) when their last minute is finished, and the adult males pack them off to bed at night.

Boys are found everywhere – on top of, underneath, inside of, climbing on, swinging from, running around, or jumping to. Mothers love them, little girls hate them. A boy is TRUTH with dirt on its face, BEAUTY with a cut on its finger, WISDOM with bubble gum in its hair, and HOPE of the future with a frog in its pocket.

He likes ice cream, knives, saws, Christmas, comic books, and the boy across the street, woods, water (his natural habitat), larger animals, Dad, trains, Saturday mornings, and fire engines. He is not much for Sunday School, company, schools, books without pictures, music lessons, neckties, barbers, girls, overcoats, adults, or bedtime.

Nobody else is so early to rise, or so late to supper. Nobody else gets so much fun out of trees, dogs, and breezes. Nobody else can cram into one pocket a rusty knife, a half-eaten apple, three feet of string, an empty Bull Durham sack, two gum drops, six cents, a sling shot, a chunk of unknown substance, and a genuine supersonic code ring with a secret compartment.

A boy is a magical creature – you can lock him out of your workshop, but you can't lock him out of your heart. You can get him out of your study, but you can't get him out of your mind. Might as well give up – he is your captor, your jailor, your boss, and your master – he is a freckled-faced, pint-sized, cat-chasing, bundle of noise. But when you come home at night with only the shattered pieces of your dreams and hopes, he can mend them all like new with just two words – "Hi, Dad!"

Once I was asked to speak at a men's breakfast at our church. I agreed; and, since I had been reading a book called *23rd Psalm from A*

Shepherd's Point of View, I chose this book to explain the welfare of sheep and the correlation between us humans and Jesus, our Good Shepherd. I made a staff and rod to use as props to explain how a shepherd uses these items. The rod was used for counting and for a weapon against wolves and other animals. Also, it was used for separating the wool to check for parasites, to correct the sheep, or to stop the sheep from stampeding by throwing the rod in front of them. If you remember in the Old Testament, Moses used his rod to initiate the plagues in Egypt. The rod was made from a root at the base of a tree with a smooth handle to fit the hand of the person who used it. The rod I made was from the root of a sassafras tree that I dug up on my farm in Jackson County. It was just the right shape and size.

First, David knew very well what he was talking about when he wrote Psalm 23. He knew that sheep could not survive without a shepherd. We humans, likewise, cannot survive without our shepherd, our Lord Jesus Christ, to prepare the way for us and to lead us. The sheep must be looked after continually by the shepherd, or they will be killed or die from their stupidity! David knew how to prepare the tablelands where the sheep traveled to get the fresh grasses, but he also knew the dangers and went before the sheep to remove any dangers before his flock got there. This is how our Lord protects and provides for us. It is said that a shepherd can walk beside a sheep with his staff against the sheep, and it is like walking hand in hand with the sheep. The staff was a comfort to the sheep and was never used for correction. The hook on the staff was for moving or handling the baby lamb so the mother would not refuse it because of our human smell.

Lee and I are both very active in our church. She works with the girls' ministries and teaches Sunday School, has served on the church administrative board, plays bass guitar or piano on the worship team, plays fiddle, and hosts the ladies' prayer group weekly. She also served as Children's Church Director for several years and was Kentucky District Missionettes Director for over twenty years. It's hard to keep up with Lee because she is so busy. She is not only smart, but she also has a lot of common sense. Often when I'm in the garage working on something, she comes up with a better way to do things.

Lee's name is Elsa Lee, but very few people know her by that name.

When the movie *Frozen* came out in theatres, the young girls at church were in awe when they discovered that her name was in fact Elsa.

In 2012, there were several church shootings, so our pastor asked me to head up a Safety and Security Team for our church because of my experience with law enforcement. Lee and I did lots of research from many sources to come up with a plan. We have compiled a library of information. We use husband and wife security teams when possible. We hold trainings at church and off-site. We have invited our local Fire Department and Police Department to come to present safety scenarios and First Aid Training.

Another of my part-time work experiences was at General Electric Factory Services on Floyd Drive in Lexington. In the shop we worked on air conditioners, freezers, and other appliances. We changed compressors, evaporators, condensers, etc., and delivered them to the owners. Don Wilson was the best teacher and friend, and he later started his own business in Irvine, Kentucky.

After this, I went to work for Gene Williamson Appliance Repair and did similar repairs as at General Electric Factory Services. We also delivered appliances for Kmart. Gene and June were very good friends of Lee and me, but we had not seen each other for several years until we met recently at a mutual friend's home at a "music jam." I found out that he and his family have entertained at Renfro Valley. He is an excellent musician. We had a great time playing music together that night. Hopefully, it won't be the last.

Let me tell you about another friend whom I have known for about 25 years. His name is Cornell Conley, but people here just call him "Cotton." He owned a transmission shop on North Broadway next to The Curb Bar. I stopped in to see him from time to time to visit or share a joke. Often, he would pull his old guitar down and sing. Sometimes we would have a jam session after he moved a vehicle out. Cotton had many friends, and he would give you the shirt off his back. Recently, Cotton closed his shop and retired. I miss him so much when I drive past the shop and realize that I can't stop and chat with him anymore. Below is a poem I wrote about Cotton that describes him quite well.

I have this friend; his name is Cotton. He's now retired but not forgotten.
Many a friend at The Curb he did feed, or anyone else he saw in need.

He was the life of the party and was ready with a song.
Or if you needed advice, just pick up the phone.
He was on the job 24/7; and if you needed spiritual
advice, he was in touch with Heaven.
He could fix your transmission or charge your AC. The
reason I know this is, he's done it for me.
When I think I'll run by and see my friend, Cotton,
I realize he's not there and I'd just forgotten.
I miss you, Cotton; you're number one; the center of
the Universe where we had a lot of fun.
He was early to rise, and I don't know when he laid down,
But every time I passed the garage he was always around.
Whether under the hood or under the frame, when
you arrive, he was always the same.
"What do you need, Babe," was all he would say, and
before you knew it, you would be on your way.

I have a friend, William Herrington, who is like my brother. Some of my firefighter friends, along with William and his dad and son, Josh, and I went deer hunting in Caldwell County. We brought home a lot of deer meat from there. William shot so many deer in one hollow that we named it "Buck Hollow." One time William was in his deer stand when a deer ran by his tree. He had just set his cup of coffee on his knee and knew that cup was going to fall, but he needed to shoot the deer before the cup hit the ground and spooked the deer. That deer went down before that cup of coffee hit the ground.

I killed a lot of deer with my 45-caliber muzzleloader, but on one occasion I had my trusted 270 rifle. The morning of the hunt I got the gun out of the case and realized I had left the bolt in my safe at home. I did this so no one could use it if it were stolen. Well, I was a long way from home, so I took my little 9 mm Glock 26 and went to the woods. A large tree was lying in a V shape in the woods, so I took my stool and sat down behind a log which was about three feet high. It would be hard for a deer to see me there. At this point, I did not have much hope of bagging a deer; but I sat enjoying the day and waited. After about thirty minutes, two men came walking through about sixty yards from me, but they didn't see me. They just walked and talked. Because of this, I figured I would not even see a deer. After about twenty more minutes, I looked up and there stood a seven-point buck! He was broadside to me. As I knelt behind that tree with my pistol aimed on him, he walked in the same direction the men had gone. He was about thirty yards from me when he stopped. I fired and he took off running over the hill. I could hear him crashing through the trees and brush. After about 100 yards I heard him fall. I sat back down to wait for another one and decided I would deal with him later. The reason to wait is that sometimes if you go after a deer that has been shot, he will jump up and run off. Therefore, it's best to just wait and let him die before you try to approach him. Now this was my plan, but it wasn't very long before I heard a voice holler, "Hey, you got one down over here." I said that I knew it and to leave it alone. A few minutes later they hollered again, and I recognized the voices as some of the guys I had come down to hunt with. And they were the same two who had walked through my hunting area. Their names were Tom Conley and Steve Muoio. I went down to my fallen deer, and they helped me gut it. I carried their guns while they dragged my deer back to camp about a half mile away. We had no four-wheelers like we do now to haul the deer back to camp.

We had a lot of fun down in Caldwell County. One time William had just bought a new pair of waterproof boots. As we were carrying a deer back to camp on a stick tied between us, he was following me and stepped into a small stream and the water came over the top of his boots! We laughed so hard we had to put the deer down and take a break. We have told a lot of good stories sitting around the deer-hunt campfire. Still to this day William and I go hunting the first day of gun season, although we do less hunting now and more story telling. We get quite excited just reminiscing.

William is a builder and is involved in many other things as well. He is one of those guys who can do almost anything and has helped me so much over the years. He has a mowing business and a snowplowing business. A few years ago, he had knee surgery and could not push snow; so, he called me to help him out when the snow started flying one day. He was at home with his cell phone and his leg propped up telling me where to go and how to push it. William is a perfectionist, and I wanted to do it just like he would. In a 24-hour period we got 23 inches of snow. Some places I had to push three times! I worked 24 hours straight and was so glad to get home.

Just to let you know how much William and his wife, Teresa, are like a brother and sister to me, they let Lee and me take their RV camper for four days to Tennessee for a Royal Rangers Territorial Event at the Davy Crockett Birthplace State Park. On top of that, he let me use his diesel truck to pull it. How many of us have friends like that?

I had a friend, Rick Crawford, in Anderson County, Kentucky, who owned property and allowed me and my neighbor, Arliss Stewart, to hunt there. He took a liking to me, and I bought a new 1986 Chevy truck from his dealership in Lawrenceburg, Kentucky. He drove me around to show me his farm and said we could hunt on any of his properties, which we did for several years. And, oh, the deer stories I could tell.

I will tell you this one story. One afternoon I was sitting in my tree stand in the fence line that ran around a field of about fifteen acres. Suddenly a tractor with a mower appeared with plans to mow the field starting from the fence line and mowing inward. I thought to myself--I'll not get a deer today with this old 45-caliber muzzleloader. But I stayed in the stand anyhow. This man mowed for about an hour and a half and had about another half hour to finish, and his tractor quit running. He jumped off the tractor and headed to the barn, which was about 500 yards away. Within five minutes a big doe came out of the tree line about 100 yards to my right. Now I was getting excited as she walked right down to the tractor to see what was going on. That's when I took aim, shot the deer, and it fell where it stood. Now as I looked around, here came another deer out of the same tree line and walked down to the spot where the first deer lay. I tried to reload my muzzleloader so I could shoot this second deer. I suppose I don't have to tell you that I was as nervous as a long-tailed cat in a room full of rocking chairs! Three things you must remember about loading a black powder gun: Powder, Patch, Ball, and in that order. Usually this is no problem, but I was shaking and that ball with a patch on it can be a bit hard to push down that barrel. I was shaking so badly that my ram rod split with the patch and ball halfway down the barrel. Needless to say, I had no way of getting the second deer; and she walked away unharmed.

I walked down to get the deer I had shot; but as I approached her, she began to move. I discovered I had shot her in the spine, and she could not get up; but she was very much alive. Remember, my muzzleloader is out of commission; and I had no way of putting her out of her misery. You never leave a wounded deer in the field, so I put my foot on her neck and tried to choke her. That didn't work so I ended up hitting her in the head with my hatchet to kill her. I figured if David could kill a giant with a stone by hitting him in the head, I could kill the deer with the blunt end of my hatchet. I field dressed her and took the meat to Burkhead Meats in Lawrenceburg to be processed. We always had them dress our deer into steaks, loin, and hamburger. That is some good eating!

William Herrington and I took our Royal Rangers on a campout to this same property. The plot of land we were camping on was not far from where I shot the deer, and the area had an old cemetery with a stone fence around it. There were two brothers with us called the Burgher Brothers, Willie and David. They went into the graveyard to look around as the sun was going down. As darkness fell, they remained inside the fence; so, William and I sneaked over and hid behind the rock wall. As they came out, we jumped out and scared them. One of them took off and ran like a rocket toward the camp, and the other one just stood there dancing. William asked him why he just stood there, and he said he was thinking what to do. When we caught up with the other one in camp, we told him what his brother had said; and he said, "I was thinking on the way." We still laugh about it.

When I left the Fire Department, I started driving charter buses for Bobby Wombles in Nicholasville, Kentucky. These are big, 55-passenger buses with TV, toilet, AC, and seats that recline for a comfortable ride. It just so happened that Col. Allen took a lot of school trips with his Junior ROTC, and he used Wombles' buses and always asked for me to be the driver. When we did this, Col. Allen always listed me as a chaperone which allowed me to go with them on flights in C-130s as part of the group. I had ridden in these planes a lot when I was in the Marines like when we went to fight in the Dominican Republic in 1965.

Col. Allen was like having my personal tour guide at Wright Patterson Air force Base in Dayton. He told me all about the different planes and especially all about the B-52 on display there. As a matter of fact, he flew out of Guam on New Year's Eve in 1969 on the exact plane that is on display. I was so impressed, and I have always looked up to him for his service to this country. He is the same one whose thumb I hit in our Sheriff training.

When Lee, my wife, retired from the Fayette County Schools, she started driving for Wombles as well. We loved driving together on trips. Sometimes each of us drove a bus; other times we shared driving the same bus. Our combined driving experiences are a whole other book, and we had lots of fun and enjoyed all the people we drove for on these trips. Frequently they asked for us to be their drivers on future trips.

I don't know if the DOT would let me get away with it now, but one time I took an out-of-town group who was staying at the downtown Lexington Hyatt Hotel, to a large Christmas party at the Kentucky Horse Park. When they got on the bus, I was dressed in my Santa suit. They could not believe their good fortune at having Santa drive their bus. I think I really made their day, or night in that case.

When I started driving charter, I tried to enjoy myself and make things fun for everyone. Three of the drivers were retired from IBM: Ronnie Ogden, Bill Smart and Rad Riggs. If we were having a long wait at the site, we called each other the night before to plan our cookout for the next day. Who would bring the grill, charcoal, hamburger, hotdogs, etc.? When we got to our destination--like Kings Island or Kentucky Kingdom--we got out our lawn chairs and started up the grill. The other drivers walked by admiring us and licking their lips. Occasionally, we shared if we had enough. We made a lot of friends, and it helped us pass the time.

After I had been driving the bus for a few years, another driver, Larry Landrum, came to drive for Bobby. Lee and I loved Larry; he is so funny and has a dry sense of humor. It was easy to pull jokes on him. Now at that time, Bobby had two Great Danes to patrol the bus lot. They were beautiful, friendly, and wouldn't hurt a flea; but their presence was intimidating. You had to be careful opening the bus lot gate because they would take off running. You had to keep them back, squeeze through the gate, and put them inside the office while you got the bus out and the gate closed before letting them out again. Sometimes they beat you to the gate, got out, and ran down the street. Then you had to drive the bus down the street and open the door. They would jump on the bus, and you could return them to the lot. Maybe they just wanted a ride on the bus. Larry was scared stupid of these dogs. It was hard for him to get to his bus because he was looking around to see where the dogs were. Well, after the dogs weren't there any longer, we still tried to scare him. One day we had a scheduled trip together. As he was unlocking the gate, I reached down and grabbed his ankle and barked. He nearly tore the lock off trying to climb that gate. We laughed and laughed. He still reminds me of that. He was a good driver and a good friend. I think he enjoyed the pranks, or I would not have done it.

Bobby Wombles, the owner of Wombles Transportation, knew his buses from bumper to bumper and top to bottom. He did a lot of his own mechanic work. If I had a problem or broke down on a run, he told me how to fix it, step by step, or he would come and work on it if we were close enough.

Bobby LOVED technology. His buses were equipped with the latest gadgets that we all had to learn to use. The most trying gadget for Lee and me was the Virtual Driver Log. Wow! No more paper log-in sheets. I took Lee on many trips I made in recent years just to log me in and out. Otherwise, I had to call Bobby at every rest area to keep me on track. You see, the DOT was monitoring these units whenever they wanted. If you were going over the speed limit repeatedly, the owner could be fined and so could you.

This reminds me of a very funny story and something Bobby might try. I was driving one day listening to the radio. A story was being related about a man who was into electronics and sound equipment. He bought a set of speakers and put one speaker in the outside toilet that was a two-holer at his church. He ran wires from the toilet to his hiding place. Soon an older lady came out to use the toilet; he gave her time to get seated and then he activated the speaker. He asked her to move over to the next seat because he was trying to paint down there. She screamed and nearly tore the hinges off the door getting out of there while trying to get her clothes readjusted. She walked quickly back inside the church. Oh, how I would love to hear her story.

This story is supposedly true, but I heard it second hand: A young ministerial student at a Bible School in Tennessee was called to preach at a church in the country. Upon arriving at the destination, he realized it was "real country"; and they had no inside bathroom facilities. Just before he was to preach, he asked an elder where he could relieve himself and was told to go out behind the church a few steps into the bushes. As he was in the process of full stream, a little old female voice from nearby said, "It sure is a nice night, ain't it, preacher." He peed on his trousers and shoes and was so startled and shaken that he left the bushes, went straight to his car, and never even said goodbye to the people. Those people are probably telling stories about how their evangelist was taken straight to Heaven.

(I have always been able to remember jokes and stories. Wonder why that was not true with my English classes?)

One time I was on a trip to Washington, D.C., and the air bags that make the bus ride smoothly burst on one side. Every time I crossed a bridge, I had to cross at an angle to keep the bus from riding rough. Bobby found a bus company in Maryland that could fix it, so Lee and I spent the day there while they put the one on that Bobby carries on the bus.

Another time in Pennsylvania the alternator went out, and I finally found a garage that would fix it. Most garages will not work on buses.

Then one time south of Nicholasville I was headed back to the garage and the engine blew. It had to be towed and never ran again. Bobby used the parts from it for that bus's twin for several years, until Lee blew that engine up in Cincinnati. Were we really that hard on them?

Coming back from a school trip to Mammoth Cave one day, Lee was following me in a bus when a tire blew out on my bus. I found a safe place to pull over and called the police to come keep us visible with their lights since we were loaded with students. The Sheriff of that county called a repair truck to come to change the tire. We were fine, and the kids were just a little late getting back to school. The principal of the school was following us in a car.

Lee and I drove these buses to Gatlinburg and were given instructions to park in a specific gated parking lot. It was nearly impossible to make the turn into the gate, but with a lot of skill and maneuvering we got in. When we finally got parked and were locking up our buses to go for a walk to town, we discovered that the way we had come in was marked "entrance only." Sometime later, as we prepared to leave the lot to pick up our passengers, it was absolutely impossible to get our buses through the exit gate. It was a double-wide exit, but in the middle of the exit there were cables attached to metal posts which were bolted into the ground. Just beyond the gate was a rock wall about four feet high. No way! We could not make the turn into the narrow alley. So, always doing as my wife tells me, I got the tools off the bus and took the metal posts out of the ground and moved them aside making the exit wider. We angled our buses so that we went through at an angle with mere inches to spare on each side. We also let a church school bus out as we left. Once out, I took the tools and put the posts back in place. Oh well, just another day on another trip in the bus. "The wheels on the bus go round and round." I should mention that we have made several trips to Gatlinburg since then, and we have never used that parking lot again. The moral of this story is that Wilbur and Lee can do just about anything; at least our kids think we can.

One time we took the University of Kentucky cheerleaders to Atlanta, and I decided I to have a little fun with them. Now, I have these "Billy Bob" teeth and "coke bottle" glasses that I wear together. As we pulled up, I had them on; and one of the parents wouldn't let her daughter get on the bus. I got off the bus and walked around to the front, and the parent asked Lee if I was for real. Lee started laughing and she relaxed a little. Finally, I introduced myself, showed them some magic tricks, and we headed out for a trip to Atlanta.

After about three days, we headed back to Lexington; and "ice" was forecast for Jellico Mountain. I wanted to get us over the mountain before it got too bad because the girls had a basketball game that evening at UK. When we got to Jellico, it had not gotten slick yet; so, we continued heading north and made good time until we got to London, Kentucky. London is at a high elevation and freezes there before other places freeze. Just north of London the road was covered with about a half inch of ice, and it was still snowing and sleeting. Going down some of the grades I drove next to the guardrails where no one had traveled, and it was not as slick there. I was driving about five miles per hour. We got the girls back to school about three hours before game time. As we pulled onto campus, they began to clap. When we stopped to let them out, I donned my "Billy Bob" teeth and "coke bottle" glasses; and they gave us "high fives" as they got off the bus. We had shown the girls magic tricks, transported them around Atlanta, and had gotten to know some of them. As I was helping them get their luggage off the bus, the lady who was nervous about her daughter going with us told Lee that her daughter had had a ball. That was her first trip with the team without her mom.

On one trip, I was driving around Knoxville in the left lane with the hammer down; and the bus just quit. My heart sank. I crossed four lanes of traffic to get to the shoulder of the road and got out to find out what happened. The fan belt had broken, and it shut the bus down to keep from burning up the engine. Bobby always carried extra fan belts and tools on the buses. As Lee held the flashlight, I changed the belt; and we were back on the road in about thirty minutes.

Another trip I took was to Atlanta with the Walker Family Reunion. The Walkers was a black family that I picked up at North Park in Lexington. They were the happiest, kindest family I have ever met. When they got on the bus, I introduced myself as "Wilbur Walker." They presented me with an orange cap that said Walker. I still have it after all these many years.

Everything went well until we got to Knoxville. The Walker family wanted to go to the mall, which suited me because it gave me a break. As they were in the mall, I walked around and noticed antifreeze running from under the bus down the parking lot. I called Bobby, and he had forgotten to tell me about the leak in the cooling hose that goes to the transmission. He said to watch the gauge and to stop if it got too hot. By the time we got into Georgia, it was getting hot, so I pulled off to get it fixed. Remember, I said previously that no one wants to work on buses. Well, that held true in this case also. So, I am on the phone with Bobby getting instructions on how to fix it myself. I had to find a parts store to buy a large hose clamp to put on the leaking hose. The leak was around the three-inch clamp that was on the bottom part of the hose. I needed to put a new clamp above the clamp that was already there.

Only half the problem was solved. I had to figure out how to get to the hose. I had to remove the floorboard from the aisle of the bus. After doing this with a light, a screwdriver, the clamp, and someone holding onto my legs to keep me from falling headfirst, I hung about three feet down in this hole. (I don't know why I am always upside down, I guess my childhood prepared me for it.) I put the clamp on and added antifreeze, and we were good to go, except that my bald head was bleeding from hitting the little metal studs that stuck out where the screws would go back in to reattach the flooring. I had grease from head to toe. It cost Bobby a new change of clothes for me because I had to throw them away. It was a miracle that we were only about an hour later getting checked into the motel than they were expecting. They were happy. When I got parked and went inside, they called and asked me to come up and eat fried chicken with them. Finger-lickin'-good!

The next morning, they visited the MLK burial site. Previously, we were allowed to park the bus along the curb; but that had changed. We had to drop them in a designated location and then park the bus. Later we came back to load them up. At the appointed time I started out of the parking lot and headed down the street. I saw smoke at the corner where I had to turn to pick them up. It was dark, heavy smoke. A restaurant on the corner was "bloomed out" as we would say at the Fire Department, meaning there was fire showing. The flames were reaching the sky. I thought, "Oh no, I have to get these people out of here before the police and fire trucks arrive." Therefore, I turned the corner and parked on the curb hoping my crowd would get on the bus; and we would be gone. Not going to happen! They were only interested in the fire like all people are. They ran past me toward the fire. Too late now!

Sure enough, the fire rigs and police arrived and blocked all the streets. A fire engine stopped right beside me and started laying hose to a hydrant about 300 feet away. It was evident they were shorthanded because the driver, or engineer as we call them, did not have an assistant engineer to assist him in hooking to the hydrant. I knew they needed water immediately, so I decided to lend a hand. I ran up the street as the hose butts were hitting the street in front of me. I got to the hydrant at about the same time he did. Just so you know, the engineer's job is to set the engine to get the water from the truck to the fire. The assistant engineer's job is to get the water from the hydrant to the truck. He must uncouple the hose, hook it into the truck, then hook a large soft suction hose to the hydrant, and turn the water on full force at the hydrant to get water into the pump.

When I got to the engine, the driver was getting out. I told him I was a firefighter and that I would hook him up. (Meaning I would be his assistant engineer). I asked him where the wrench was, and he pointed to a compartment. I hooked him up and headed back down to the fire. I wanted to see how this Atlanta Fire Department operated. They did a good job and had the fire out in a short time. It was on the evening news, and the restaurant was a total loss; but they stopped it from spreading to nearby buildings. I did not realize it then, but to the Walker family I was beginning to look like "some kind of a hero."

After touring Atlanta for the rest of the day, we headed to Stone Mountain which is just northeast of Atlanta. Lee and I once ate in the Westin Hotel Restaurant, which revolves as you eat. We could see Stone Mountain from the restaurant. Stone Mountain gets a lot of visitors because you can ride the train around the base of the mountain, hike up or take the tram to the top, and then watch the laser show at night. Well, on this particular day there were very few vehicles in the parking lot. I parked next to another bus, then took the train ride and rode the tram to the top of the mountain. I was having a great time with my new family, the Walkers. Now a problem was developing that I was not even aware of. I did not realize the Walker family was not staying for the laser show that night. When we started down the mountain, there were cars, buses, campers, and anything else you could drive covering the entire parking lot. Some of them were parked up in the grass between the trees. It looked like my bus would not be able to get out till after the show. Now I guess I am bragging, but I am a pretty good driver. As a matter of fact, at the Fire Department another firefighter and I tied for the best score when we did a driving test in the fire truck. Like I said, I think I can drive backwards better than I can forward.

This reminds me of the story I heard about a bus driver who was stopped for speeding in Ohio by a young highway patrol officer. The bus driver told that young whippersnapper that he had driven farther backwards than he, the cop, had driven forward. I don't know if the cop heard him or not. How could a cop take him to jail and leave a busload of people sitting on the side of the road.

Back to Stone Mountain--when we got back to the bus, we were able to maneuver out of there by getting two cars and a bus to move. The bus driver then helped by directing me from outside the bus, and inch by inch we turned that bus around. We were out of there. My passengers gave me a sitting ovation and said I was going to be their driver in the future. I always entertained them with magic tricks, poems, jokes, and riddles when we were not moving or stopped for breaks.

I must tell you this now--Bobby Wombles is a good, honest, smart, and wonderful boss to work for; but he was easy to pull a joke on. One time I had a school busload at the University of Kentucky for a football game. Back then we did not have communication radios in the school buses, so we used hand-held radios that we carried with us when we were off the bus. I had parked the bus in the loading dock where security had directed. Some fans had extra tickets and invited me to the game. I sat way up in the nose-bleed section, and Bobby called me on my hand-held radio to ask if I was with the bus. I said, "No." He asked me where the radio was, and I told him I had left it on the bus. He told me to go get it or it would get stolen from the bus. I told him I was talking to him on it, and we had a big laugh.

As I mentioned earlier, magic tricks have been a big part of my life since I was seven years old when I figured out how to do a trick with a little square box with six colors on it. Preacher Bill Holman taught me this at Youth Haven Bible Camp. I have worn out several of these boxes and have carried them all around the world, even Vietnam, and very few people have figured it out. Since then, I have added many other items to my collection of tricks and illusions. You will seldom find me when I don't have at least a couple of items in my pockets, on my wrist, or up my sleeve.

I do tricks with ropes, rubber bands, and cards. I can make things disappear or cause things to change places, cards float in mid-air, and I can even pull a rabbit out of a hat. One trick uses a guillotine, and I invite a member of the audience to place their hand in the guillotine.

The kids are always brave until they see me slice a carrot in half. The looks on their faces are priceless. I hear comments like, "No way am I putting my hand in there." Now, I don't know if girls are not as smart or if they are braver than boys. Maybe it is that the girls don't listen when I'm explaining about what is going to happen while I am putting on my latex gloves and asking the parents if their insurance policy is paid up. Then, as I am reading the disclaimer, the boys all sit down and only the girls remain. Lee and I have a lot of fun with these tricks, and we call it "White Magic" instead of black magic.

I'm always ready to pull a trick out of my pocket at a restaurant or anytime I see boys and girls who would understand and be amazed because I just love to see their smiles. If a person is really interested, I will break the rule of a magician and explain to them how it works. Hopefully they will take up this fun and exciting hobby. Anyhow, most of them can be found on the internet and YouTube.

Lee has always sung in church and played the piano and organ. Now she plays the bass guitar and the fiddle. Lee has a great ear for music. She reads music AND plays by ear. Now that I have started singing, she has a hard time keeping me on tune especially when I am trying to start a song that I don't know very well. I play guitar and sing. We jam with a bunch of our friends several times a week but have not gotten to jam very often since COVID-19.

Sometimes we set up our Bose sound system on our front porch and have a singing for all who want to come and listen. We have had "Music at the Whites' House" several times. We put the musicians on the porch, and our friends and neighbors bring lawn chairs and sit under the shade tree. We just "jam" away! Years ago, we had "Breakfast on the White House Lawn."

We have made lots of friends through our music. Some of them are professionals, some of them should have been, and some are just plain mediocre, like us. We have a group that we sing with sometimes called "Sam Clark and Friends" --Sam, Ben Taylor, Bill and Cindy Breeze, Lee, and I. Cindy plays the keyboard, bass, acoustic guitar, dobro, and other instruments and has written several great songs. Sam Clark is also a singer and songwriter and plays in the group with us. Sam was invited by a songwriter's organization in Nashville to move there to write for them, but he would have had to leave IBM. That was not in his plans. We sing at churches, homecomings, and any other events where we are invited. A few times we have even gotten paid! We have so much fun. People really seem to enjoy it but probably not as much as we do. We are so sad that Bill passed away from complications from COVID while in Florida. He was the kindest, most gentle, and talented man I ever met. He sang funny songs, country songs, and sweet gospel, like "The Old Roman Soldier" and "These Are All Mine." Then, the last time we sang together, he sang "Don't Let the Old Man In," written by Toby Keith, which was a tribute to Clint Eastwood.

One time Sam had an operation on his nose. (I told him to keep it out of other people's business.) We were scheduled to sing at a church homecoming. Sam had a big white bandage that covered his whole nose. So, I thought I would have a little fun and made a bandage for Bill and me with double-sided tape. It looked just like Sam's, so Bill and l stuck ours on just as they were introducing us. It was a good way to start the singing. The audience laughed and laughed. It was a great icebreaker, and they rewarded us with an awesome dinner after church--my kind of people, for sure.

We have recently changed our group name to "Singing Patriots." We have fun with that, also, since all the men in the group are former military.

Sam built a studio behind his house so that we could come play with other musicians a couple of times each month. We had a lot of super good pickers and singers. Sometimes we had ten or twelve pickers/singers, and other people came to sit and listen. Sometimes there were fifty people filling the room to capacity!!

We also played at Jim and Marie Howard's house. Not as many people or pickers, but we had just as much fun. We always enjoy their hospitality, and usually it is a different group of pickers at each location. Jim's musical ears are so sensitive that he can tell you if your string is out of tune before you even touch it . . . well almost. I try not to sit too close to him because I fear I may have a string not exactly in tune. Sometimes he or Ben Taylor tell me that I need new strings. Most people wouldn't have the nerve to tell you that. I appreciate all the help I can get. It takes a true friend to do that.

There is a Christian TV station in Beattyville, Kentucky, called WLJC. We have sung there several times, and that is a real experience. We have learned a lot but still have a long way to go!

On Monday nights we play at JR Carty's house, and sometimes we have the same musicians and sometimes we have different people. We really feel like family with all the groups we play with. Lee read somewhere that people who play music or sing are less likely to get dementia at an early age. We are going with that.

Thursday nights we play at the home of Charlie Cutshaw in Georgetown. Usually this is a different crowd as well. Before COVID, Charlie always set up a singing at the Georgetown College each year where we had food and singing that lasted all afternoon. Charlie is one of the nicest, most generous people you will ever meet. We love him, too, just like family. Every time we go to sing at Charlie's, he expects me to tell some jokes about him.

One of the jokes goes like this: Charlie had a big pond on his farm that was close to Georgetown College and the students loved to swim there. One day Charlie drove his tractor out there to check things out and found some girls sunbathing. When they saw Charlie, they jumped in the pond and left their clothes on the bank. Quick-thinking Charlie had a bucket in his hand and said, "Girls, don't mind me. I just came down to feed the alligators!" Charlie, you devil, you.

One day was payback for Charlie. Sometimes he liked to take a dip in the pond to cool off on a hot day, so he stopped the tractor and placed his clothes on the grass. He had barely gotten into the water when the girls came to swim. What can he do? The girls see his clothes in a neat stack on the bank and go sit on them. He asked the girls for his clothes, and they laughed and laughed. Now Charlie was frantic. What can he do? He felt with his feet and found an old enamel wash pan on the bottom of the pond. He covered his "privates" with it and walked up the bank. He was angry and started giving the girls a piece of his mind. He says, "Do you know what I think?" One girl said, "You probably think that pan has a bottom in it."

Somewhere along the way we met a man named Steve Norman. He is a fine mandolin player and singer, and he also plays the guitar and Jew's harp. He is a farrier by trade and is well known in the racing world. They fly him to Florida to shoe horses for the races there. He is an all-around nice guy.

Lee's nephew, Steve Robinson, owns Century 21 Advantage Realty in London as well as several other towns, including Lexington. He chartered a bus from Wombles Transportation, and Lee and I took him and his staff to Keeneland for the annual Kentucky Century 21 Awards on a Wombles coach. Steve Norman went out of his way to give a special presentation for them on how to shoe a horse for a race at Keeneland. He brought the horse right up next to the fence where they were standing. This was very profitable because some of the group bet on the horse that Steve had shoed for each race. Did you know the farrier is listed on the program for each race? I did not! They were betting on Steve's horse regardless of the odds. Most of them won money. Steve had given me a five-gallon bucket of used horseshoes. All of them were unwashed and some still had nails and poop. Our plan was to clean them up and then take them to Steve in London to give to his agents later, but they wanted them like they were---poop and all!!! Way to go, Steve Norman! You and your used horseshoes made their day even better.

Bobby Wombles also helped make their day special by placing their Century 21 Advantage Realty logo on the bus door. When people saw our group getting off that bus, they were really impressed, and our group was so proud. By the way, Steve's Advantage Realty group took top honors that night, also.

We are so proud of Stephen Robinson. He has done so well and is still in the National Guard. During the Iraq war, he was awarded the Joint Service Commendation by Paul Bremer of the US Department of Defense. Steve served as Lieutenant Colonel with the Coalition Military Assistance Training Team from July to September, 2003. He was tasked with organizing and supplying the New Iraqi Army; devising a budget; securing weapons, uniforms, and other supplies; arranging training for soldiers; and overseeing large cash transactions. He oversaw millions of American dollars along with Saddam's seized riches to build the new Iraqi Army. He was later promoted to Bird Colonel.

Steve Norman has a band called "Shades of Grass" that travels and plays different venues, and sometimes Lee and I go to listen.

There is a song called "Come on Down to the Farm" that I sing that is controversial in some venues. It talks about farms and the reproductive facts concerning animals. We got it from a DVD from a pastor in Tennessee, who sang the song. Steve wants us to sing it every time we get together. We were sitting in the audience in a small town where Steve and his band were performing. He saw us in the crowd and said, "Hey, Wilbur, come up here and sing my song." We began singing the song. By the time I got to the chorus, two men came up to the front with their thumbs down and yelling in disagreement with the words of the song. Steve told them to leave or go sit down. There was no more turmoil, and the crowd seemed to love it. We got a big, long applause when we finished. The next day Lee and I were in Pennsylvania with our great grandson, Austin, to see Sight and Sound Theatre when I got a call from Jess Craig, our friend; and he said, "Wilbur, was that you?" I said, "Was what me?" He said the local evening TV news and newspaper carried the story about someone being called out of the audience in a nearby town to sing a song that offended someone. I said I guess it was me! When we hung up the phone, I called Steve to ask about it. He said there was someone offended by the song, but he got them straightened out. He said he won't do that gig anymore. I didn't know I was offending people; I just thought that is life. People offend me all the time, but I figure that's their right. Lee has a saying she uses a lot, "Just get over it." So, I guess I agree with her. By the way, Steve's calls to perform gigs increased 99 percent after that episode. Just recently he told us this continuing part of the saga. A horse-owner friend of his had a mare he named "Steve's Mandolin." She ran a race but did not win. This horse delivered a filly that he named "Band from Midway." Steve has become notorious since that fateful night.

The next week we were on a bus trip to the Pike County coal mines in Eastern Kentucky, and I told a guy about the incident. He said, "Was that you?" It was in the papers in Eastern Kentucky, too.

Another funny song we sometimes do in private settings was written by Bryan Lewis in Ohio, and it's called "I Think My Dog's A Democrat." Bryan gave us permission to print the words to the song, and part of it goes like this:

163

I think my dog's a Democrat, and it breaks my heart to have to say an ugly thing like that. But there's a big old pile of evidence that all points toward the fact — my dog might be a democrat.

I pay for all his health care, and I buy everything he eats, I provide him with a place to live just to keep him off the streets, but he just acts like he's entitled, even tried to unionize the cat. Yeah, I think my dog's a democrat.

He chewed up the constitution that I keep on display, and every time Benghazi's on TV he looks the other way. I know he's a liberal even if he won't admit it. He pooped on my living room rug and tried to tell me George Bush did it!!

This song and several other Bryan Lewis songs are available on YouTube.

Several years ago, we made a CD with Jim Howard and some other musicians. Lee played the bass guitar, and I played the guitar and sang. It was recorded in Paris, Kentucky, at Barking Dog Studio. We were a long time getting that CD because the squirrels chewed the wires in the attic that were used to put it all together. That is a true story. We still laugh about the squirrels.

Later we became friends with Winston May, *Studio 353,* in Frankfort, Kentucky. He has a studio in his basement and uses top-of-the line equipment. He has an awesome ear for music and plays the steel guitar and lots of other instruments. Winston knows how to mix the music and make you sound good. We were fortunate to get to meet him. He played in the band at a place called "The Barn" in Burgin, Kentucky. Sometimes when we went to The Barn to hear the singing, Tommy, the owner would invite Lee and me to do a song or two. Once Lee got to play her ukulele bass, and once she played Tommy's bass. Sometimes I did a magic trick or two. All their musicians were fantastic. They never lacked for accomplished musicians. It was a great show every time.

Winston made and mixed our gospel music CD entitled *Just Good Gospel* with twelve songs. He recommended a man in Berea named Mark Law who owns *Shedhouse Productions* and performed at Renfro

Valley at the time. He wrote the play "Christmas in the Valley." He was just as professional as Winston. He not only duplicated the CDs, but he did the graphics for the cover as well.

A few years later, for our 50th wedding anniversary, Winston and Mark made our *Just Good Love Songs* CD. We were equally satisfied with this one as well. We have had hundreds of people tell us they never heard CDs that were better mixed. We have considered making another CD.

A few years ago, after leaving the Sheriff's Department, there were some stumps in my yard that needed grinding. A friend of mine, William Herrington, recommended Jim Barker for the job. After he ground the stumps, I told him we should team up. He looked me in the eye and said, "OK." Now I'm in the stump-grinding business, and we have been together for about sixteen years.

I have learned a lot from Jim, but I still have a lot to learn. I think Jim is one of the best landscape artists around, and he knows so much about trees and plants. He owned two garden centers and gained knowledge by reading and by hands-on experience. He is from the old school, and many times I find myself agreeing with him.

One time when Jim had a garden center in Paris, he cut a guy off on his way to work; and the man pulled over in front of Jim and blocked him, jumped out of his vehicle, and confronted Jim, but not before Jim grabbed a shovel out of the back of his truck. Jim said, "Let's get this over with; I'm late for work." The man said, "You don't fight fair," and jumped back in his car and left. The lesson here I guess is to just carry a shovel or don't cut people off!

I don't know why Jim doesn't weigh 500 pounds because Barb, his wife, is a cook second to none. When food is served at their church, her food is the first to disappear--according to Jim. She is like an angel, and the other day I told her I saw wings beginning to sprout on her shoulders.

Jim and Barb met in North Middletown, Kentucky, when he fell in love with this beautiful young girl dressed in her pleated cheerleading skirt when she walked out onto the gym floor at North Middletown High School. I guess their love must have taken, because, July 29, 2022, marks 70 happily married years. That is surely a record.

Jim is one of the tightest people I know, but he learned to be thrifty as a child growing up in Johnson County in Eastern Kentucky. I told him one day that he wouldn't give a dime to see an ant eat a bale of hay. Then he told me this story that proves it. He said he was in a store one day; and a tall, skinny man came in talking to the people who were standing around. The man bet another man $1 that he could pick up a quarter off the toe of his shoe with his teeth. Now Jim was thinking he had false teeth and would take them out and pick up the quarter that way, but that was not the case at all. Jim said he leaned over and picked up the quarter with his teeth in his mouth! That would have impressed me. Wish I had seen it. The man then turned to Jim and bet him $5 he could climb a tree backward. I would have paid a lot of money to see this feat, but Jim was unimpressed. I'm not sure why, but Jim used to cut a lot of firewood so maybe he knew how to climb a tree that way.

One day Jim and I made $230 grinding stumps. We saw a woman on a corner asking for help, and I said, "Jim, let's give her the $30." I can't believe he agreed, but we don't do that very often. Most of these panhandlers around here make more money than we do.

We've backed that stump grinder through a few fences that we have had to repair, and that really cuts into our profits. We've had to fix a few yards that we have messed up a little bit, but we try to make every customer happy--even if we must go back and redo some roots we have missed. It has been a good time working with Jim. Jim and Barb and their children are considered part of our family. Lee and I really love them.

Back in the 1980s I drove a school bus for Fayette County Public Schools part time in the mornings. I was a firefighter at the time; and when I got off duty at 6:55 a.m., I went to the school bus garage on Liberty Road and filled in wherever needed.

One day I had middle school kids. As I was driving through the project area, these kids were screaming, hollering, jumping up and down, and going wild. I slammed on the brakes to get their attention. I said, "You all need to settle down and be quiet because I can't hear myself think." While I was screaming at them, a parent came out of her house and asked if her child was giving me a hard time. I said, "No, ma'am, it's all of them." She said to let her know if hers does not behave. That was the end of that, and I never had any problems after that.

Another time I was on Haley Pike off Winchester Road. There was a long driveway that went into a subdivision. When I got there with the bus, there were three small children standing and waiting for the bus. I opened the door and they got on the bus. As I started to leave, I looked up the lane and about 200 yards away I saw two high school kids from Bryan Station High School just sauntering toward the bus. I sat there and waited for them. Very seldom did I get assigned the same route two days in a row, but the very next day I was on the same route. When I pulled up to this stop, there were the same three little ones waiting. As I looked up the lane, there came three more older ones just ditty-bopping down the road. I closed the door and took off. At Briar Hill Elementary we let some kids off and picked up others. Now these three boys beat me to Briar Hill School. They boarded my bus and mouthed all the way to my next stop, which was Bryan Station High School where these boys were enrolled. After I listened to all their cursing and threats on my life, we went to the principal's office. We got things cleared up quickly, and they apologized after listening to the Assistant Principal, Jim Komara, who was a volunteer firefighter whom I knew. I'm sure this had no bearing on the matter. I just hope the regular driver saw a change in the promptness of the kids for the bus.

One time in the 70s I was driving a Roadway tractor on North Broadway near Seventh Street. A school bus heading north on Broadway ran up on the curb, onto the sidewalk, and stopped just before hitting a telephone pole. I could see that a student had the driver's head bent back over the rail behind his seat and was choking him. I stopped my truck and ran over to the door of the bus as another lady who had seen what was happening approached the bus at the same time. I asked her to call the police. As I stepped up on the bus, the boy was still holding the driver. I told him to let him go but he hesitated. Then I think he saw how serious I was because I was just getting ready to hit him right on the tip of his nose. He turned the driver loose, ran out the back door of the bus, and disappeared. What is strange is that no one on the bus knew who he was. The bus driver was transported to the hospital, and his glasses were broken, also. When the police found the boy at Bryan

Station High School, he was suspended for three days. I thought they should have gotten his attention in some other way to deter this type of behavior. He probably loved being out of school for three days. I'm glad I did not have to hit him because I would still be in jail today.

Not all bus driving experiences were bad, and I must tell you about this wonderful thing that happened to me. One morning I was driving a bus with a full load of kids going to Russell Cave Elementary School on Russell Cave Road at Ironworks Road. Don Cope was the principal at Russell Cave Elementary and was a good friend of mine. His twin brother, Lonnie Cope, owned the barber shop where I worked part time. Just before we arrived at the school, one of the kids on the bus got sick and vomited on the floor and on a couple of seats. I went into the school to get some cleaning supplies to take care of the situation. When I asked the secretary for the supplies, she said, "Let me help you with your problem." Now this got my attention because I couldn't believe that this lady would jump in to help a bus driver who was torn up like a dollar watch. This beautiful lady got all the supplies, came on board, and took care of cleaning my bus, and helped make it presentable for the next run. I could not thank her enough for what she had done for a stranger. I did not give her a medal which she deserved, but the next day I took her a bouquet of flowers. The Bible does say that we will entertain angels unaware, and I believe she was one of them. Mr. Cope told me she is one of the most wonderful people he knew.

Lee and I have been married 57 years, and for our 50th Anniversary, our daughter, Connie, and her husband, Glenn, and our granddaughter, Jamie, hosted a huge celebration at our church. We had so many friends and family and guests. It was a wonderful time. We left the next week for a two-week drive out west. We headed to the Pacific Ocean. We made a winding trail through the Dakotas, Wyoming, and into Yellowstone. Then we headed north toward Washington state via Montana. When we came out of Yellowstone, there were severe forest fires in the western states. The smoke was so thick, you couldn't see the sun. The natives said that this was not normal at all; so, after travelling into the edge of Montana, we got concerned when we saw on the news that people were abandoning their cars and walking away from the fires. We did not want to be stranded there, so we turned south and called the Excalibur Casino in Las Vegas and made reservations for the night. We drove 900 miles that day and arrived late that night. We were tired but glad to be out of the smoke. You could still see smoke that far south.

We booked a Pink-Jeep tour to the Grand Canyon and the Hoover Dam for the next day. When we got on the Pink Jeep, there were only two other women on the tour with us. They were from Australia, so we had our own private tour guide driving the Pink Jeep. It was fabulous. Our guide was the best. He carried water in his backpack; and every time we got off the Jeep, he handed us a bottle of water. He said that when he met us on the trails, he better see us drinking water! He told us that whenever there was a medical emergency out like that, it was almost always due to dehydration.

We spent a couple of hours at Hoover Dam and went down to the bottom of the dam to view the workings of the turbines and engines. They explained the maintenance procedures. It was a great tour. We got back to the hotel late and walked through the casino to a restaurant. We were so very tired that we did not even stop to spend one quarter! Rooms there are so reasonable. They think you will spend your money gambling with them, and most people do. They lost big time on us.

After that, our son-in-law, Glenn, and Connie took us and our grandson, John, on a cruise to the Bahamas. We all got along great and had fun on and off the ship; however, one of the ship's motors went out and we hobbled back to Miami and that caused us to miss the most important port of call, the Dominican Republic and San Juan. I was so disappointed because I wanted to go back and relive part of my military tour of duty, and I hoped to find the girl who had come in and shared the three-hole toilet with me in the Ambassador's compound.

Over the years we have gone to visit Branson, Missouri, several times. We love the music shows and took in two or three shows each day. There is so much to do. On one trip we visited the "Shepherd of the Hills" music show and play in the amphitheater. While we were there, we visited the Vigilante Zip Line tower. We never intended to ride it but after looking around, we decided it might be okay; so, we did. The ride is 2,370 feet long with speeds of 50 mph. I don't think Lee is afraid of very many things so I knew she would be okay. She was on one line, and I was on another line and just a little bit in front of her as she was taking a video of me all the way down. This thing was so long and fast that it gets hot; and when it comes to a halt at the bottom of the mountain, it sprays water on the moving parts of the cable to cool it down. We got a little wet at the same time, too. Lee will drive a tractor, drive the charter bus, operate the stump grinder, push snow with the plow, climb a tree to rescue a cat, and deer hunt with an AR-15. What more could a man want. Remember the riches.

To celebrate our anniversary this year I wrote Lee the following poem:

As I look at the years gone by,
I wonder how you fell in love with this guy.
How you have stuck with him through thick or thin;
Our love is still alive like it was back then.
We have enjoyed life to the fullest with joy and laughter,
While all the time preparing for the hereafter.
We could have seen a lot of things and gone a lot of places,
But the love and joy we have can still be seen on our faces.

In May, 2020, Glenn's daughter, Megan, and her husband, Joe, presented us with twin girls, Molly and Marie. These two great granddaughters are a special blessing. For their second birthday, I helped Austin make them very small butterfly necklaces. I wrote a poem to go with the necklaces. Now we just learned that in late October 2022, we will become great grandparents to a little boy, Jackson Glenn Shatterly!

The Butterfly
The butterfly is a good example of being born again,
Because it starts out as a caterpillar and then turns into a beautiful butterfly.
This is what happens to us when we accept Jesus as our Savior.
For you see, if you are born once, you die twice;
but if you are born twice, you die once.
These black, red, and white beads are a good example
of this, because our sins were black,
but the Blood of Jesus washed those sins away and made us white like snow.
I hope you can use this again when you are asked about this beautiful butterfly.

Lee's mom still lives in Jackson County, Kentucky, and we visit her often. Remember, she loved me before Lee did. Recently we were there with other family members installing a TV in the kitchen which she had requested. She wanted to sit in there and watch TV, drink coffee, and watch the deer and turkeys in her back yard and pastures. So, her grandson, Steve Robinson, and his wife, Lisa, bought a flat screen TV for her. They asked me to help install it; and, of course, I was glad to help. After we got it installed, we had to get the cables down through a hole in the floor to connect to the existing lines in the basement. As Steve and I were headed to the basement, I saw our great grandson, Austin, standing there and I asked him to feed the line down through that hole in the floor. He jumped back and said very adamantly, "I am not feeding a 'lion' through that hole." He was so serious, and we laughed so hard we almost fell down the basement stairs.

I wrote a poem for Austin called "The Wash Rag."

A washrag is a tool you can use when it's dry
To wipe the sweat from your face with a sigh
You can use it to wash dishes in the sink
You can clean up a mess as quick as a wink
Now Austin uses a washrag to wash his skinny frame
Morning and night is all the same
Wring it out I said one day
Hang it over the shower door; it's ok
But Austin has a plan I don't understand at all
He just lays it in the corner of the tub in a wet little ball
I guess I have to live with this, though many times he's been told
This is such a little thing, and this boy is made of GOLD!

Epilogue

I never imagined in my wildest dreams that I would ever write a book. I didn't set out to write. I have so many experiences and so many stories to tell that several people prompted me to write it down. Lee has a cousin, Rosita Shields, whose husband is an author. Jim has several published pieces including several children's books and poems. One of his children's books is *Starbird's Special Gift*. I love that story, and I wrote a poem for Jim and named it "A Feather." I put it in a Lucite desk frame and placed a tiny red feather at the bottom. I hope you order the book to understand about the feather. It's a keeper.

> *A feather, I said with a smile.*
> *Why, I've had these since I was a child.*
> *But for you, I'd pull and I'd pluck*
> *'til there's nothing left but skin;*
> *Why, for you, I'd do it again.*
>
> *Cold and hungry you found me that day.*
> *What might have happened I cannot say.*
> *Now I can soar in the skies above*
> *But this feather's yours because of your love.*

Another author I am impressed with is Marvin Sullivan from Falmouth, Kentucky. He wrote a book, *Back Yonder*, which tells stories from his past. It has just enough humor, and the stories are interesting and just the right length. I liked the way it was put together, so I asked his permission to use his format. We went with his publishing company, Authorhouse.

My life has been so full and exciting. I hope you can now understand why I used the unusual title. It depends on what you call RICH. If it is about wealth, we missed out on that; although, God has blessed Lee and me to have a comfortable lifestyle. We are RICH in friendships, beautiful family, health, and God's blessings galore! We go through all the heartaches every other human endures, but our faith in God tells us the Son/Sun is always shining beyond the clouds. Thank you, Jesus. We try to live every day to honor Him; not ourselves. What makes life so wonderful is that I was born twice. Think about it; you will find it in the Bible.

I hope this book can make a difference for the better in your life, and like me, you thank God that we are Americans.

There is a poem I am particularly fond of. It is called "The Man in the Glass" (author unknown). I will leave you with this, and I hope you can say that you also are truly **RICH.**

> *When you get what you want in your struggle for self,*
> *And the world makes you king for the day*
> *Just go to the mirror and look at yourself*
> *And see what THAT man has to say.*

> *For it isn't your father or mother or wife*
> *Whose judgment upon you must pass.*
> *The fellow whose verdict counts most in your life*
> *Is the one staring back from the glass.*

> *Some people might think you're a straight-shootin' chum*
> *And call you a wonderful guy*
> *But the man in the glass says you're only a bum*
> *If you can't look him straight in the eye.*

> *He's the fellow to please, never mind all the rest*
> *For he's with you clear up to the end.*
> *And you've passed your most dangerous, difficult test*
> *If the guy in the glass is your friend.*

You may fool the whole world down the pathway of years
And get pats on the back as you pass.
But your final reward will be heartaches and tears
If you've cheated the man in the glass.

Printed in the United States
by Baker & Taylor Publisher Services